Praise for *Tri*

Trivium 21c is an educational masterpie[illegible]
education in a hugely entertaining form. [illegible], *Trivium in Practice*, is a collection of essays by practitioners who explain how teachers might make real the theoretical model of the trivium. Tom Sherrington's practical application of the trivium in an inner-city London comprehensive school is brave, true and inspirational. Mike Grenier's short history of trivium-related pedagogy at Eton is a delight. Carl Hendrick's contribution is typically intellectually challenging. The final chapter, which details Dr Jonathan L. Taylor's work at Cranleigh School, should give hope to all of us who yearn to educate our students, not school them to be qualification hoop-jumpers. This is a book whose time is now, which reflects the courage of practitioners who can rightly call themselves educators.

John Tomsett, Head Teacher, Huntington School

With *Trivium 21c*, Robinson did something rare: he wrote something new about education based on ideas that were centuries old. With *Trivium in Practice* he brings that into the classroom. Together, these two books should be compulsory reading for any teacher entering the profession, and every teacher within it.

Tom Bennett, founder of researchED and behaviour advisor to the DfE

Trivium in Practice is a great book that forces us to think about what students need to learn at school. Building on *Trivium 21c* which successfully yokes medieval and 21st century ideas together, this field book lets us see how practitioners from different sectors have successfully combined the trivium with their own beliefs and traditions. We need students and teachers who speak and think and write with the clarity of philosophic understanding which Robinson shows so well. Teachers will immediately be able to see how they can adapt and use these ideas.

Professor Bill Lucas,
co-author of *Educating Ruby: what our children really need to learn*

We all grow tired of hearing this or that book is a 'must-read' for all interested in education. Most of the books are, to be honest, ephemeral. But this book is different, about the profoundest idea in education, and how to mobilise it in today's schools.

Sir Anthony Seldon, Vice-Chancellor, The University of Buckingham

Anyone hoping for a how-to guide or a template on 'doing' the trivium will be disappointed; this is not that. Instead, Robinson has edited a collection of thoughts, discussions and approaches on how grammar, dialectic and rhetoric might be brought together and adapted to fit in any setting.

David Didau, education blogger, author of *What if everything you knew about education was wrong?*

By embracing the tension in the discourse between education's traditionalists and progressives, Martin Robinson brings the liberal arts trivium into the 21st century. This latest instalment presents a valuable compendium of real-world examples of practice that teachers and school leaders interested in nurturing autonomous learners will find invaluable.

Graham Brown-Martin, author of *Learning {Re}imagined*

TRIVIUM
IN PRACTICE

II

Tom Sherrington
Sam Gorse
Nick Wells
David Hall
Mike Grenier
Nick Rose
Carl Hendrick
John L. Taylor

Martin Robinson

First published by

Independent Thinking Press
Crown Buildings, Bancyfelin, Carmarthen, Wales, SA33 5ND, UK
www.independentthinkingpress.com

Independent Thinking Press is an imprint of Crown House Publishing Ltd.

© Martin Robinson 2016

The right of Martin Robinson to be identified as the author of this work has been asserted by him in accordance with the Copyright, Designs and Patents Act 1988.

First published 2016.

All rights reserved. Except as permitted under current legislation no part of this work may be photocopied, stored in a retrieval system, published, performed in public, adapted, broadcast, transmitted, recorded or reproduced in any form or by any means, without the prior permission of the copyright owners. Enquiries should be addressed to Independent Thinking Press.

Independent Thinking Press has no responsibility for the persistence or accuracy of URLs for external or third-party websites referred to in this publication, and does not guarantee that any content on such websites is, or will remain, accurate or appropriate.

The email on paages 47–48 is reproduced with kind permission of Carole Baily.
The extract on page 80 is printed with kind permission of Maurice Holt.
Materials from the Eton College Library archives on pages 99–101 reproduced by permission of the Provost and Fellows of Eton College.

British Library Cataloguing-in-Publication Data
A catalogue entry for this book is available
from the British Library.

Print ISBN 978-1-78135-243-4
Mobi ISBN 978-1-78135-255-7
ePub ISBN 978-1-78135-256-4
ePDF ISBN 978-1-78135-257-1

Printed and bound in the UK by
TJ International, Padstow, Cornwall

To all the Philosopher Kids.

Acknowledgements

Firstly, thanks to the tireless dedication and patience of those who contributed to the book: Tom Sherrington, Sara Stafford, Andrew Fitch, Marie Deer, Becky Hulme, Ruth Ramsden-Karelse, Sukhi Dhillon, Sam Gorse, Nick Wells, David Hall, Nigel Matthias, Nick Barnsley, Mike Grenier, Nick Rose, Carl Hendrick, John L. Taylor. To all the other people who supported them in the writing of this book. To all at Crown House for their continued belief in the trivium by bringing this project to fruition. Finally, to those early reviewers whose comments have helped in the shaping of this book.

Contents

Introduction

> 'During our first meeting we discussed the scope of this seminar, and we decided that we should limit our study of the medieval Latin tradition to the first three of the seven liberal arts—that is, to grammar, rhetoric, and dialectic.' He paused and watched the faces—tentative, curious and masklike—focus upon him and what he said.
>
> Williams, 2012 [1965]: 136–137

Trivium – where the three ways meet. The three ways are grammar, dialectic and rhetoric. Dialectic is sometimes referred to as *logos* or logic. These three ways formed the basis of the medieval liberal arts curriculum and were the core of a good education from ancient Athens through to our contemporary liberal arts institutions and schools. Rather than being 'planned', the three arts were drawn together by chance and tradition – yet, at their core, lies an uneasy truce between truth, critique and articulate opinion. This difficult relationship is the key to unlocking understanding, creativity and independent thinking and learning. It is the key to an education of 'character' – and, when drawn into the teaching of subjects, it is the key to great teaching and learning, not as an imposition but as part of the tradition of teaching and learning itself. The trivium isn't a gimmick to be imposed on to a curriculum; it is a tried and tested approach to education. It is in the 'blood' of teaching and learning:

Knowledge, Questioning, Communicating

Or, as Sir Anthony Seldon put it in *The Times* (Tuesday 16 February 2016):

> Education in medieval times was based on the 'trivium', with students learning facts (grammar), the ability to argue (logic), and how to communicate (rhetoric).

When one expands this into grammar being foundational knowledge and skills; dialectic being questioning, thinking and practising; and rhetoric being to express oneself beautifully, persuasively and articulately in any form, then one can begin to see how great teaching has these three things at its centre.

When one sees rhetoric as reaching out to the world and bringing things together, and dialectic as examining, thinking, looking at differing viewpoints and ways of doing things and developing one's opinions and individuality, and grammar as being the best that has been thought, said and done, one can start to see how it might work in the classroom.

The teacher holds the baton of valued knowledge. They pass this baton on to a child, and the child and teacher hold the baton together for some time, tussling with and arguing over the valued knowledge to reach some understanding of it, while developing the child as an individual – not swamped by valued knowledge but equal to it. Finally, the teacher lets the baton go, for the child to run with it, to express *themselves* in their studies, to reach out to the community, and make their own way, developing their own character and thinking. The opportunity is there for the child to grow and add to the best that has been thought, said and done. As C. L. R. James (2013: 119) put it:

> The end towards which mankind is inexorably developing by the constant overcoming of internal antagonisms is *not* the enjoyment,

> ownership, or use of goods, but self-realization, creativity based upon the incorporation into the individual personality of the whole previous development of humanity. Freedom is creative universality, *not* utility.
>
> James, *Modern Politics*

The pupil is expected to develop both as an individual and as a member of their community. As the basis of the liberal arts, this is an education for 'freedom'. This is not an education that expects children to follow a preordained pattern, but one that ensures they have the wherewithal to join in with what Michael Oakeshott referred to as 'the conversation of mankind ... perhaps we may recognize liberal learning as, above all else, an education in imagination, an initiation into the art of this conversation ...' (Oakeshott, 1989: 39).

It is the conversational classroom and the adventures that might be had within this space that are at the heart of the trivium. Debate, dialogue, reading, writing, critical thinking, creativity, self-expression will all feature in this classroom. The importance of memory, of 'knowing', is the base of this, but it is only part of the story. From knowing, through practice and critique, to flourishing, simple ways of thinking about the curriculum can unlock complexity due to the unique tensions between the three arts of the trivium.

There is no one 'right' way to 'do' the trivium: it is a tradition that can be adapted to time, to places, to different habits and ideas. This is its joy – and also its annoyance. How much easier it would be for a school leader to 'buy' a way of doing it and inflict it upon her staff, students and parents.

The trivium is a glorious human accident: contradictory, yet it is the art of education and engages teachers in the art of being educators. Just as each great artist learns from a tradition and refashions it, adds to it, disrupts it, so do the teachers who have contributed to this book.

I don't agree with everything written here; there are things I would want to do differently, but on their canvas, in their school, each contributor is creating and re-creating trivium education in their own way. I hope you will be suitably inspired to do the same in your own home, your classroom, or in your own school.

References

James, Cyril Lionel Robert (2013) *Modern Politics*. Oakland, CA: PM Press.

Oakeshott, Michael (1989) 'A Place of Learning'. In Timothy Fuller (ed.), *The Voice of Liberal Learning: Michael Oakeshott on Education*. New Haven, CT: Yale University Press, pp. 17–42.

Seldon, Antony (2016) 'We've degraded education in the hunt for A stars', *The Times* (16 February).

Williams, John (2012 [1965]) *Stoner*. London: Vintage.

Chapter 1

Teaching: the Great Debate

One way to think about how the trivium might work in a classroom is to think about how it can be used to teach a topic. For this task I have chosen a simple idea that involves a debate to which there is no clear right or wrong conclusion. If we were to follow trivium principles, we would expect to do something along the following lines:

> Grammar: The facts of the topic. Dialectic: The argument(s). Rhetoric: The pupil's expression of their own opinion about the topic.

Notice here that the opinion comes at the end of the process. I often get into trouble by saying we're not interested in pupils' opinions ... until I add the *yet*. For example, I used to teach something and ask pupils' opinions about it straight away. This yielded responses that, though they may have been varied, were often instant reactions to something 'unknown'; something which often results in a negative or not altogether enthusiastic response. The trivium works in a different way: this class, and teacher, are only interested in educated opinions, and welcome a broad range of opinions, as long as they are backed up by good knowledge of the debate and encourage pupils to bring their own self to bear within that conversation.

In many subjects there are texts that open themselves up to scrutiny and dialogue. Competing theories and ideas, intractable problems (both political and cultural), competing views of history, even business ideas and how best to manage a football team offer up opportunities where there is no clear-cut answer. Sometimes a single text has a debate running through it, or is open to a variety of interpretations. In theatre, the 'grammar' might be the script and also the work of the dramaturg finding out the facts about the play and its themes. The 'dialectic' would then come in through an investigation into the grammar – learning the script, practising, workshopping and rehearsing the script ready for the final 'rhetoric', or performance of the play to an audience. Even though the script is the same, no two productions of the play will be the same. The process opens up interpretations, and the same should be said for the process of learning in the classroom.

The text could be by Shakespeare, or by Virginia Woolf; it could be about the Civil Rights movement or about the Falklands War. It could be a discussion about the merits of 4-4-2 vs 4-2-3-1 in football, or a look at whether Darwin's theories are useful in economics. Whatever your subject, there will be some opportunities to open up a text (or texts) to debate.

A Vindication of the Rights of Woman by Mary Wollstonecraft might be such a text. Straight away there might be a problem here, because much of what is included in this text might not be as controversial today as it was when it was published in 1792. Therefore it might not be a good text to choose for this approach – but that is not the point. The trivium can help people understand texts by testing out the strength of an argument within them, so that at first look they might superficially agree with them, at the end of the process they might know why they agree, and, what's more, they might be able to bring their thoughts to bear in other scenarios. Wollstonecraft's tome might be looked at alongside the work of John Locke and Jean-Jacques Rousseau. It could be looked at through the lens of contemporary debates about nature vs nurture, and also through contemporary feminist critiques about patriarchy. By learning the arguments, children would get a good grounding in the depth of the debate.

The next stage would be to get children to explore the debate through a technique known as a *dissoi logoi*. Through this method a pupil would be encouraged to look at two sides of an argument – or more – and be asked to write a single piece that gives equal weight to the 'rightness' of both sides. This is the process through which instant opinion is 'shelved' and stronger, educated opinion begins to be formed.

> The grammar: learn about the text and its background. Learn about opposing viewpoints. The dialectic: bring those opposing viewpoints together in a piece of writing, weighing up the different facts and opinions in a *dissoi logoi.*

This could then become the basis for a Socratic Circle. The pupils sit in a circle, with the relevant text in their hands, and they discuss the text, responding to questions from the teacher and from each other. The point is to look at and explore ambiguities in the text, to test out its logic and, maybe, to seek to challenge it. The importance of this process, again, is the warding off of 'opinion', using instead 'evidence' (as written in the text) to justify opinions that each pupil may have. The teacher can play devil's advocate and/or be a stickler for the use of 'facts' as evidenced in the text(s).

> The grammar: knowledge of text(s) and other relevant information. The dialectic: a dispassionate look at the argument, drawing from knowledge (the grammar). A testing out of this argument through questioning.

This can be followed by formal classroom debates focusing on a question: 'this class believes ...' and is one way of opening up the third part of the trivium, rhetoric. One can also begin to see how each part of the trivium overlaps with other parts. Pupils can write speeches and learn them. The teacher can tell pupils which side of the debate they will be speaking for beforehand – something which truly tests the ability to understand, use evidence and persuade others. Once the debate has been conducted, the final 'rhetorical' task could be set, which would be an essay stating the true 'educated' opinion of each child. This could be read out, open to debate, or remain in essay form to be questioned via a viva, or responded to in more conventional ways.

There are various ways to structure a piece of rhetoric and numerous methods that can be employed. What follows is a 'classic' structure which can be taught to pupils to improve both their spoken and written word work.

First, introduce the 'five parts of rhetoric'. These are:

1 Invention

2 Arrangement

3 Style

4 Memory

5 Delivery.

Then explain what each one is. Again, I want to keep it simple.

1 *Invention*: this is the content of your speech and the drawing together of your 'evidence'. It includes ethos, pathos and logos, the three musketeers of rhetoric. Ethos is your credibility. Pathos is the shared emotion between you and the audience. Logos is your use of reasoning and logic. This usefully models critical thinking.

2 *Arrangement* (the six parts of oratory): this can be a lesson in itself! I believe that if you teach this well, then not only will your pupils speak better, they will also be able to write essays better. Below is the 'classic' order for a speech, and it makes a great scaffold for an essay too:

   i You begin with the *exordium* (or 'hook'): this should catch the audience's attention and it should also be central to your narrative.

   ii Next comes the *prothesis,* where you present a short history of the subject that you are going to be talking about.

   iii This is then followed by *partitio* (division): here you make the points which are uncontroversial and then the points which are contested.

- iv Then *confirmatio* (proof): here you state the reasons behind your thinking.
- v Next is the *confutatio* (or refutation): you go on to refute any opposing argument.
- vi Finally, *peroration,* where you sum up the argument passionately and not by presenting a simple review.

3 *Style*: should the style of the talk be low, medium or grand? Low style is 'down with the kids'; medium is probably the best for day-to-day speaking; but it would be good to introduce the 'Grand Style' of great oratory to see if pupils can lift the audience to a higher level through their eloquence.

4 *Memory*: as a drama teacher, this doesn't worry me. I think sometimes it is good for pupils to memorize their speeches. It isn't always necessary, but sometimes it can lift the presentation. Speaking from memory mustn't be robotic, however; it must have *sprezzatura*: in other words, the speaker must allow their thoughts and ideas to inhabit them, so that they seem to spring fresh from their mind!

5 *Delivery*: you will need to work with your pupils on their delivery. This includes the use of space, positioning, posture, presence, communicating the feelings of honesty and truth, gestures, facial expressions and – crucially – the use of their voice: volume, pitch, tempo, pause and inflection are all important.

What you have just read is a classic trivium approach to studying a text or texts. However, I must emphasize that this process is not just one that fits snugly with the humanities and the arts. Every subject has its grammar; it has its logic; it has the need for practice and areas to analyse and debate; it also has its opportunities to 'perform' – whether on the sports field, in an exam or in the answering of questions.

The trivium is a helpful way for a teacher to think about the art of teaching, and can help in the design of a curriculum, when one is looking to achieve balance, increase student involvement and understanding, and develop creativity, independence and critical thinking (alongside the need for good academic knowledge and investigation).

Reading maketh a full man; conference a ready man; and writing an exact man.

Francis Bacon

Chapter 2

Philosopher Kids at Highbury Grove School

Tom Sherrington

Sara Stafford, Andrew Fitch, Marie Deer, Becky Hulme, Ruth Ramsden-Karelse, Sukhi Dhillon

Tom Sherrington has been the head teacher at Highbury Grove School (HGS) in north London since August 2014. He had previously worked as a teacher and school leader in a number of different types of school, in a career that started in 1987.

Highbury Grove is a mixed comprehensive of 1,200 students in Islington. The school has a diverse intake spanning the full range of social and ethnic backgrounds and pupils have a wide range of prior attainment on entry to Year 7. A very high proportion of students speak English as an additional language, and over 70% receive Pupil Premium funding.

In this chapter, some Highbury Grove teachers write about how the trivium came to influence their thinking about curriculum and ethos. Each member of staff has their own perspective on the value of the trivium in shaping their thinking as teachers and school leaders, and on the ability of the trivium to influence a wide range of different approaches. Their commitment to the idea of the *philosopher kid* shines through.

In this chapter we talk about how *Trivium 21c* has influenced our thinking about teaching and learning and the curriculum at Highbury Grove. More than that, it has influenced our vision for the education we want to provide, and the kind of young people we want to develop at our school. From the outset I want to be clear that we are on a journey that has only just begun. Many of the ideas we've explored are in their infancy and, if you came to visit, you might not yet be dazzled by the knowledge and rhetorical fluency of philosopher kids in every corridor and classroom across the school. Not yet.

It's also important to stress that we're not entirely starting from scratch. We're building on some strong practice in various departments, and we are fortunate to have a staff body made up of enthusiastic, knowledgeable teachers who have had plenty of success in the past. To some extent, the power of *Trivium 21c* is that it brings coherence to a set of ideas that already make sense to most teachers, albeit elevating them to a higher plane of philosophical thinking. As a school that is fiercely ambitious for our students, we have now embarked on a gradual, deep change process that we hope will take the conceptual principles inherent in the trivium – the three arts of grammar, dialectic and rhetoric – and make them a tangible reality for every student in the school.

Already we have learned that, to give shape to the principles, you need some signs and symbols; some set-piece events and devices to move things forward. Even as I write, things are changing, new ideas are developing, and the trivium is finding form in classrooms across the school. However, we are conscious that the rhetoric is always far ahead of the reality. It's important to keep things in perspective as the story unfolds. This isn't the territory of quick fixes or top tips for teachers; it's about taking some deep and powerful ideas and making sense of them in the complex world of an inner London comprehensive school where pretty much anything can happen. Above all else, the process is one of raising our sights and believing that every young person from every background deserves an education that can lead to fulfilment, enjoyment, enlightenment and success in the modern world. I'm convinced that the trivium provides a framework for creating a school that can genuinely deliver on that promise – and that is what we're trying to do.

The notion of children becoming philosopher kids is highly emotive for us, and has great symbolic power. At Highbury Grove we get fired up by the idea that every child could be a philosopher kid. Over 70% of our students receive Pupil Premium funding; many of them experience disadvantage at a high level every day and face massive barriers. When we talk about these ideas, we are sincere in our mission to include every single student. A trivium-fuelled curriculum is for everyone, not just the elite band who fit the philosopher kid mould more comfortably through the advantages they have inherited. It's the idea that the trivium represents an entitlement for all that inspires us. Every child can be a philosopher kid; that's the dream we are chasing.

I first encountered *Trivium 21c* in January 2014, several months before joining Highbury Grove School as head teacher. At the time, I was interested in the debates around knowledge and skills, and the long-running competition between traditional and progressive ideas in education. While recognizing the different views in these debates, I've never felt it should be necessary to pick a side. Martin's book brought a clarity to this discussion. Through the model of the trivium, it is possible to conceive of a framework where traditional values and progressive ideals can coexist; where knowledge and cultural capital matter and where skills are interwoven with the content. Martin's book demonstrates that we shouldn't – and indeed can't – resolve the tension in these debates: what we can do is harness that tension to create something exciting.

Arriving at the school in September, I suggested that teachers and leaders should read *Trivium 21c*. I told them it was the best book on education that I'd ever read – and that remains the case. It can be risky to build something up to that extent, but I was immediately encouraged by the staff reaction. My senior leadership colleagues felt that grammar, dialectic and rhetoric resonated with them in their assessment of the various challenges our students were encountering in their learning. We shared the view that the Ofsted-driven culture – and the implicit prescription for what constitutes an Outstanding education – was stifling teachers' imagination, and wanted to build our own framework from the bottom up. We decided to make 2014/15 a year in which we would develop a Highbury Grove School

Framework for Teaching and Learning for ourselves, taking inspiration from anywhere and everywhere.

As Head, I had a significant role to play. Without question, my personal conviction and enthusiasm for Martin's book and the ideas in it was a driving force in bringing the trivium to Highbury Grove. But it wouldn't have happened if others hadn't also felt the same. Several enthusiasts emerged very early on: the Head of Art, the leader of our Outward Bound programme and various other subject specialists could immediately see the relevance of the trivium to their area of the curriculum. I wrestled with wanting to lead from the front, compelling staff to embrace the trivium, and the softer approach of setting out the ideas and allowing everyone to make sense of them in any way they could. In the end, it was a bit of both.

We put together a series of twilight continuing professional development (CPD) events where we explored the trivium with staff. We kicked the whole thing off at a pre-Christmas staff meeting where every member of staff was presented with a ribbon-bound copy of the book. We bought 120 copies at a very good rate! This had symbolic power as well as practical value. We wanted people to know we were taking this seriously.

In the first session, we outlined the concepts in the book via a carousel of workshops based on each of the three arts. In my session on grammar, I was struck by how much this resonated with people. We looked at a series of texts dealing with a range of topics – from sport to history and literature. It was immediately obvious how much knowledge is assumed in reading each text; how much cultural information is taken for granted; and, crucially, how far teachers need to go to fill in the knowledge gaps for every child so that they can access the intended meaning of the text. The need for grammar was an easy sell. The same was true for rhetoric. We all recognized that our students often lack the confidence and skills required to express their ideas fluently. Within his ideas about dialectic, logic and logos Robinson writes that: 'the word logos emphasizes a higher level of knowledge, skills, and experience.' The universal logos (Robinson, 2013: 136). For us this established the need for children to have authentic, hands-on learning experiences. There is value in seeing things at first hand, in experiencing the physical world beyond the classroom and in exploring concepts by being part of them, not merely looking at them from a distance.

We were delighted that Martin Robinson himself agreed to join us as part of a consultancy process. This included him giving some presentations, but also involved undertaking a series of one-to-one consultations with key curriculum leaders. Over the next few months, teachers began exploring the ideas in the trivium through CPD sessions and in departmental discussions, and we built some momentum. Martin fed back from his consultations so that we could keep up with the discussions. Here is a flavour of some of Martin's discussions with curriculum leaders:

Drama

Looked at answering the question, 'Why teach drama?' Focused on the art, rather than the social aspects of the subject. Looked at creating a grammar of drama at Key Stage 3 to both support development at Key Stage 4 and 5 as well as support the appreciation of the art for those who choose not to study it further at exam level.

Recommended the introduction of a notebook at Key Stage 3 so that pupils see writing as an intrinsic part of the subject.

Looked at how drama skills can be used to strengthen rhetoric across the school, especially in presentations.

Modern foreign languages (MFL)

Looked at how to build MFL so that pupils grow in confidence as users of languages.

Discussed how to help pupils remember their learning as well as get the chances to use languages they have acquired.

Recommended interleaving of topics and regular low-stakes testing.

Looked at grammar, and wondered whether verb use, rather than just lists of nouns that fit into a topic, might be a way forward.

Looked at possibilities for dialectic and rhetoric in the language being studied.

Recommended regular low-stakes short tests to help remembering.

Science

Looked at the idea of threshold concepts and how/when they are taught and that, once learned, the expectation of the grammar used and concepts understood need to build on what is now 'known'.

Looked at experiments and discussion coming after understanding of concepts in order to reinforce or confound expectations.

Discussed the rhetoric of science and the idea of pupils becoming 'consumers of science' and 'readers of science' through the media and other outlets; the need to be critical and see beyond the headlines.

Discussed the rhetoric of science along the lines of Christmas Lectures. Giving opportunities for older children to present to younger children (once quality has been assured) concepts that reinforce the knowledge for the older children and introduce, or help explain, such concepts to the younger ones.

Maths

Looked at the grammar of maths and how you can break down any topic into its component parts.

Revisit knowledge covered in regular low-stakes testing.

Interleave topics.

Have children teach younger ones once expertise in a topic is established: rhetoric.

Look at establishing an atmosphere where children are ready to explain maths to each other once mastery is established – seminar atmosphere at a certain point.

Humanities

Looked at the narrative of history and how concepts recur throughout history as well as feed understanding of topics – e.g. 'empire' is a concept worth learning about because it recurs in different forms throughout the study of history. Roman Britain, Nazi Germany, American Hegemony, USSR and Putin as well as themes of colonialism (and hegemony).

Looked at narrative through character and conflict – how timelines can help, and how lessons can refer back to previous learning in different topics as a historic web is woven.

RE: looked at the relationship between RE and philosophy; mooted my idea of the history of thought.

Beyond our trivium discussions, I undertook the process of observing every member of staff teach a lesson during my first year. I produced a document called '90 Lessons' that attempted to capture the essence of the best practice in the school, alongside some recommendations for improvement. A core group of senior leaders and teachers had the task of pulling together ideas and concepts from '90 Lessons' and the trivium into something coherent. We decided that, for the purposes of our documentation and for future reference, we needed to clarify our understanding of the elements of the trivium. Martin helped by summarizing sections of his book and, together, we produced the following:

Trivium 21c: *A Framework for Constructing our Curriculum and Pedagogy*

The trivium of grammar, dialectic and rhetoric formed the basis of a classical education from ancient Greece up to Shakespeare's time at school and beyond. In the 21st century, it remains a powerful framework for formulating ideas about learning, the curriculum and pedagogy. At Highbury Grove, we have embraced these ideas to guide and inspire us in all that we do.

Martin Robinson has written these short sketches of the key concepts for us:

Grammar: Knowledge, skills, tradition, authority, discipline, hierarchy, the culture, what makes this art unique? The relationship between the 'master' and her apprentice is central, with the teacher as expert and the pupil as needing to know. The body of knowledge: the best that has been thought, said and done. Connecting ideas, the importance of the whole narrative, and also how the subject connects with others, beyond its own confines.

Dialectic: Exploration, critical thinking, analysis, philosophical enquiry, thought, reasoning, creative, scientific and mathematical thinking, encouraging dialogue, debate, argument, questioning, the individual pupil gradually coming into view and finding themselves flourishing through practice and self-discipline. Humour, wit and playfulness. Authentic experience.

Rhetoric: Communication, turning outwards to the world, persuasion, product, performance, community, relationships, caring, love, responsibility. Writing, speech, challenge to exist and 'be' in a public space, giving of yourself to others. Parenting, leading, emotionally controlled and mature, thoughtful, empathetic – ethos, pathos and logos.

In practice, this means that we actively seek to create conditions in our schemes of learning and lesson planning where the trivium comes alive, with more familiar associations for communication with students and parents. Our simplest distillation of the trivium is expressed in our Framework as follows:

Grammar = Knowledge

The direct transmission of knowledge and explicit teacher instruction

Retention and recall: teaching for memory; learning by heart; low-stakes testing; knowledge for its own sake; repetition and practice

Explicit teaching to build cultural capital; explicit teaching of subject-specific terminology and the skill of reading different texts

Dialectic = Exploration

Opportunities to debate, question and challenge

Opportunities for hands-on authentic experience and experimentation

Opportunities for enquiry, analysis, critical evaluation and problem-solving

Rhetoric = Communication

A strong emphasis on structured speech events to share and debate ideas with others

Opportunities to perform, to make things and to showcase the products of learning

Opportunities to contribute to the discourse about the values shared in the school and the wider community

Philosopher Kids

At various points in *Trivium 21c*, Martin refers to the concept of philosopher kids. It's the idea that, to some extent, provides the greatest inspiration for staff. Rather than quoting from different sections of the book, we asked Martin to write something for us that pulled his ideas together:

> *At Highbury Grove we believe that children need to feel they are on an adventure in the pursuit of wisdom through which they develop as lovers of learning in all its rich variety. We believe in the importance of knowing, exploring and communicating; we believe in building a strong community where every member of the school bears responsibility for the strength of our institution.*
>
> *Plato talked about the need for philosopher kings and queens; at Highbury Grove we wish to enable our pupils to become philosopher kids.*
>
> *Philosopher kids are curious to know; they question, and they can lead as well as follow. Philosopher kids like to feel, to think, and are notable for their eloquence and ability to take part in the 'great conversation' through which they make a contribution to our common life.*
>
> *Philosopher kids engage thoughtfully in dialogue and argument; they appreciate and make beautiful things; they are confident when grappling with difficult ideas; they love music and also seek out space for quiet reflection and contemplation.*
>
> *We challenge all our pupils to become cultural polymaths, true 'renaissance people', able to flourish as individuals as well as realize that they have an important role to play in enabling their family, friends and community to flourish as well.*
>
> Philosopher kids: know; explore; communicate. (The Highbury Grove School Framework for Teaching and Learning, n.d.)

The final document, The Highbury Grove School Framework for Teaching and Learning, was the ultimate product of all of this thinking. Below, Sara Stafford, Assistant Head and Director of Research at the school, describes how it all fits together.

Sara Stafford, Assistant Head and Director of Research

Teaching and Learning, and the Trivium

Teaching and learning (T&L) is central to everything we do every day, and to everything that we are working to achieve. When writing our new teaching and learning policy, we knew that we had to get it right, and that's why we took a whole academic year to build our vision. This visual, based on the school logo, captures what we came up with. It's a working document that will grow with us year on year.

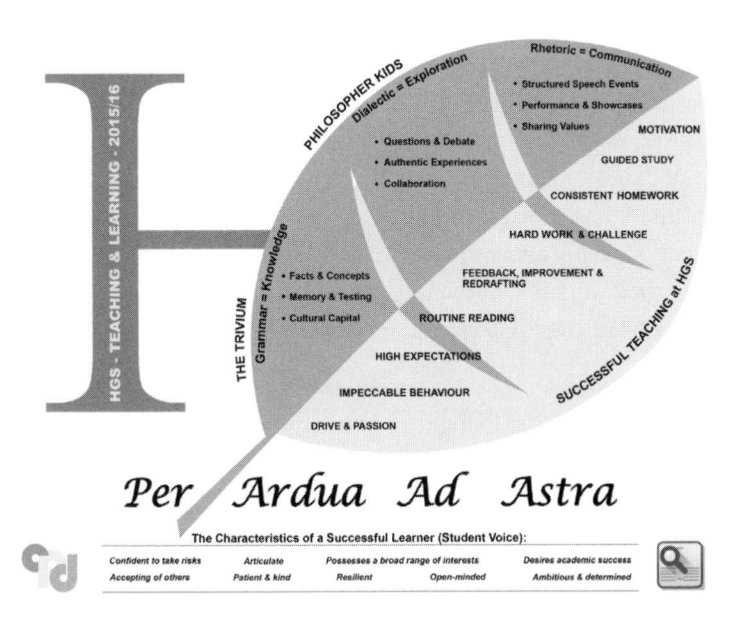

The contrasting two halves of the leaf represent our two main sources of input for our model. On the right are the key elements that we hope to engender in our pupils; the ingredients of 'successful learners'. These were collected in conversation with subject teachers, through the departmental review process, and from Tom's '90 Lessons', during which he observed every member of staff and was able to feed back an overview of what we do really well already, and what we might need to improve. We want our learners to develop high expectations for their own learning and to expect to work hard, hand in a good standard of homework and behave impeccably as the norm. Ultimately, we want them to understand, through guided study and support, how to become independent, self-motivated learners.

On the left side of the leaf, our focus on integrating the trivium becomes clear. Successful HGS learners are philosopher kids; they know, explore and communicate. We have thought carefully, as a school and as individual subject teachers, about what each element means to us and to our students. For us, 'Grammar' has become 'Knowledge' and is made up of the facts and concepts we want our students to know. In our new assignments, there is a strong focus on memory, interleaving and regular testing to embed this knowledge. And here, we have also thought about 'cultural capital' and the information we must give our students to allow them the best chance at success. In a similar way, 'Dialectic' is represented here as 'Exploration', and this is where our planning will factor in plenty of opportunities for students to explore, debate and question their learning through authentic experiences and collaboration. Finally comes 'Rhetoric' which is 'Communication'. We want it to become normal for students to speak, in a range of different contexts, regularly and with confidence. We want them to perform and present their work to parents, teachers and each other and, in doing so, to build and share our HGS values.

Our motto, *Per ardua ad astra*, ties the two sides of our leaf together: it is through a rigorous and thoughtful approach to planning, as well as a clear focus on the kind of learning we want to create, that we will, 'through hard work' get 'to the stars'.

The Framework and the leaf diagram can now be found all over the school and on the school website. Our goal now is to bring it all off the page and into the day-to-day experience of every student.

Our thinking on the trivium has run in parallel with the development of the concept of assignments. In order to create a clear structure for learning in every subject for every year group, with clear deadlines for work completion, we've broken everything down into assignments: units of work where all the key tasks and the key elements of the content are laid out. Staff quickly seized on the possibility of linking assignments to the trivium, and that is what we've tried to do. Each assignment sheet highlights the key knowledge content in the unit – albeit in a highly summarized form – they also include the key aspects of exploration (or dialectic) and the key opportunities for communication (or rhetoric).

Martin is always urging us not to make artificial divisions between the three arts; he always stresses that they form a Venn diagram of overlapping, interconnected sets of ideas and experiences. That resonates with several curriculum leaders, who have found it impossible (and ultimately pointless) to decide whether, for example, a debate counts as dialectic or rhetoric. Each subject has developed assignments with a structure that makes sense within the parameters of the subject discipline. However, when taken as a whole, there is a very strong trivium influence.

Perhaps the most significant influences are in the area of grammar and rhetoric. Teachers are now talking about the key knowledge requirements in a given unit and are developing more activities that allow students to encounter and retain knowledge, separate from other exploratory, dialectic processes. Students are being given a lot more short knowledge tests and, increasingly, we're discussing the prior knowledge required to access texts.

Our work on rhetoric has been accelerated significantly by our engagement with the trivium. This has come at a good time. With the demise of the Speaking and Listening component of the English Language GCSE, there might have been a risk that speaking opportunities would fall away. However, rhetoric has come to the rescue. To push this forward, it became apparent that we would need a champion; someone who could operate beyond the confines of one department. The obvious candidate was

Andrew Fitch, a post-holder in the English department. Andrew has a track record of promoting debating through the English-Speaking Union, and is currently the coach for the English national schools debating team. Below, he highlights his thoughts about putting the trivium into practice through spoken literacy.

Andrew Fitch, 2 i/c English, Director of Spoken Literacy

It appears that the conventional wisdom was that students should, having been 'taught' something, simply write it down: the classic model being the 'PEE' paragraph (Point, Evidence, Explain). Through this teachers were meant to be able to create a classroom atmosphere in which learning was engaging (how?), and be able to test the students' development of both knowledge and skills (thin). Moving away from this simplistic, one-size-fits-all structure, and using the three-part trivium structure, I have utilized debate, in a variety of forms, to ask students to intellectually engage with relevant material through being forced to attack and defend various aspects of the knowledge (grammar) that they have been given, whether this is the themes of a text, or the way in which a writer has used language to persuade their audience.

Through argument generation and speech creation, students dialectically engage with the material, developing a familiarity with it beyond the simple stating of facts (the 'feature safari', as I have heard it called). This forces students to reconfigure the grammar they have taken in, to think about how it applies in different contexts, and different aspects they can use to argue about it, thus deepening their understanding. That Steinbeck has his characters refer to Curley's wife as a 'tart' is an interesting piece of information: however, the argument that he is presenting 1930s America as a sexist place in which women were often called 'tarts' shows not only that knowledge has been taken in, but that it has been understood through its re-contextualization.

Through using debate students are then able to rhetorically show what they have been able to glean from the material through structured, measured speech acts, conforming to clear rules and processes that, having been clearly established beforehand, allows students to express their understanding verbally. This frees those for whom writing is more difficult, and develops the quality of spoken literacy of all students involved.

Andrew has produced this excellent guide for staff and is working with individual teachers and departments to put these ideas into practice:

Spoken Literacy and Rhetoric in the Classroom: a short guide for teachers

This guide is designed to provide teachers with a set of 'handy hints' to encourage the development of spoken literacy within their classroom, and to provide assistance when seeking to create more substantial speaking events in lessons.

As part of the whole-school T&L agenda, we are trying to ensure that effective spoken literacy and rhetoric play a significant part of our scheme of work (SoW), not as add-ons, but as a key aspect of everyday practice.

When asking students to speak in lessons, remember:

- There is no reason not to have the same high expectations of speech that we do of any other work they do – if it is not good enough, have them do it again! Whether this means repeating a whole presentation, or simply resaying the same answer but grammatically correctly, or more loudly, demand excellence.
- Praise and feedback are just as important when responding to a piece of spoken work as they are to written or any other type of work.
- Creating a culture of speech in your classroom means having everyone doing it, not simply those that are willing – do not let students 'hide'.

- Give students a warning about when you will ask them to speak – let them think of what to say. This both increases willingness and the quality of what is said.
- Try to avoid giving them anything to hide behind, whether it is a book, PowerPoint or the protective 'I don't want to speak' response.
- Give students room to rehearse, or practise, before they present.

Introducing spoken literacy and rhetoric – small activity ideas:

- Make your plenary a small presentation (tell students in advance they'll be doing it) about what they have done that lesson.
- Have a rota of who will have to explain to the class what you did last lesson (tell students in advance to prepare for their turn) – a simple but effective starter.
- Have students answer standing up, explaining not just what the answer is, but *how* they came to it.
- Give students a 'stance' to take in a discussion before you start, and have them defend that position, rather than just giving their opinion.
- Have students 'track' their pair or group discussions in note form as they go, then present the discussion that they had as feedback.
- Give students extracts that they can read in advance so they can become familiar with them and present them from memory – or at least with a clear idea of what is to come (this can be within or across lessons depending on the size of the extract, and how well you want them to know it).
- Make students present what they have done to the class, explaining the choices they made (e.g. why did they use that simile, or that artistic technique on that part of the piece?).

When planning for extended speaking activities, give clear success criteria, as you would for any other activity. Just because students talk naturally, this doesn't mean that they will naturally know how to speak effectively. For example:

- Look at your audience when you are speaking
- Know in advance what you are going to say, so you do not read from notes
- Only put notes on a PowerPoint (if you use notes at all), not the whole presentation
- Speak loudly and clearly
- Use standard English
- Give your speech structure (the 'rule of three': have three points/ideas; have an introduction, main body and conclusion; say what you are going to say, say it, say what you have said!)
- Stand up straight, with hands out of your pockets – adopt an open stance

Give students time to both prepare their presentation and, crucially, to practise it (whether as explicit homework, or with each other in class).

Set the expectation that insufficiently prepared/performed presentations will have to be redone until satisfactorily completed.

You could spread out your presentations over a longer period of time:

- Give out the 'task' at a set point then have a rota of who will present/perform their part week by week (perhaps something around, but not directly part of, the SoW they are working on)
- Give out the same task but on different material across a unit as the unit develops (tailored to the specific area of the SoW you are working on)

Or have a set role for others in the group while presentations are going on:

- Give students the success criteria and have them assess each other (perhaps providing what went well (WWW) and even better if (EBI) feedback, or choosing a 'winner')
- Give students specific areas (such as body language or tone) to focus on and give feedback on

RHETORIC ROAD-MAP: YEAR 8

Department/Activity	Autumn 1	Autumn 2	Spring 1	Spring 2	Summer 1	Summer 2
	English: Students to take part in a formal debate about human rights	Geography: Written and redrafted persuasive speech on 'Britain's Energy Future'	Geography: Formal Debate: 'Is fair trade really fair?'	Science: Presentation on light	Geography: Pedagogic presentation on various ecosystems	English: Students to perform modern adaptation of a scene from 'A Midsummer Night's Dream'
	Geography: Formal presentation using PPT on weather report	History: Spanish Armada Puppet Show performance	Science: Formal presentation on the history of the periodic table	P&R: Formal debate on General Dyer and the Amritsar massacre	English: Pedagogic session on an aspect of SPaG	Science: Formal presentation on difference between animal and plant cells
	Drama: Original performance – no notes performance of duologues	P&R: Formal presentation: comparative religion: Bar Mitzvah and Confirmation	P&R: Students present without notes on the links between Sikh beliefs and practices	English: Whole class performance/recitation of 'Half Caste'	Drama: original performance – no notes monologues	P&R: Formal presentation: The peace movement in Vietnam
	P&R: Formal recitation of student-composed poems on importance of identity and covenant in Judaism	Maths: Pedagogic presentation Design a Logo: Explain how to find the area and perimeter of their logo	English: Spelling Bee		P&R: Structured discussion: 'Contemporary conflict – what are religious views?'	
	Computer Programming: Clock interface design presentation	Computer Programming: Using Logo or Scratch write and present a user guide				

- Ask students to prepare questions related to the presentation that they will deliver at the end of the presentation
- Have the student presenting set a quiz or questions that must be answered using the information in the presentation (or simply set a few questions relating to the task before they speak)
- Try to experiment with different types of presentation: debate, pair discussion or interview (chat-show style), recital, monologue, public reading of work, etc.
- Rather than have the students wedded to a PowerPoint, make them learn a speech, or piece to perform. Students will use any 'crutch' they can to make themselves feel secure, and PowerPoints are a sure way to stop any audience interaction or learning of a speech!

Our discussions have led us to the conclusion that we can't simply push these ideas out and hope that they take hold. We don't want to leave it to chance or to the vagaries of the school timetable to determine which lucky students get the teachers who have the enthusiasm to promote spoken literacy in their lessons. We are now in the process of putting together a more structured approach – a rhetoric road-map. This will look something like the figure on page 28.

This is just for illustration. The plan is to have at least one subject making a planned contribution per half term for every year group throughout the school. This will help teachers to focus on delivering those opportunities, knowing that they fit into a bigger overall plan.

At a whole-school level we have also introduced the custom that students routinely contribute to assemblies. Student leaders now have a role in every assembly, even if this is just introducing another speaker. Previously, this was rare in the school, and only a few students had the confidence to do it. We've run a series of training sessions and have already made a good start in changing our culture. We want to normalize the idea of speaking to an audience, and promote the idea that talking in a formal manner using standard English is an important life skill for everyone.

The following contributions from different members of staff illustrate the way the trivium has begun to have an impact in different areas of the curriculum.

Marie Deer, Head of Sociology

The Trivium in Practice: Sociology

Sociology GCSE was introduced to Highbury Grove in 2014. The principles of the trivium helped to inform the design of the new course, providing the subject with discipline-specific pedagogy and a rigorous set of learning goals. Crucially, the trivium reminds us that subjects must be taught as disciplines, and this raised key questions before the planning process began: how can we teach students to think like sociologists? How can we teach students to engage with critical sociological discourse? How can a course combine passing exams with developing young sociologists who appreciate the intricacies and uniqueness of the subject?

These are important questions. Below are the aspects of the trivium we have used to begin to address them, develop teaching and learning in the subject, and create a strong subject identity.

Grammar

The range and depth of knowledge required in sociology is tremendous. It has been useful to rethink the balance between grammar, dialectic and rhetoric. Consequently, we decided to embed opportunities to explicitly teach students how to memorize and retrieve large sets of information. We paid particular attention to helping students develop the architecture required to store complex concepts, studies and language in their memories, using strategies such as the memory palace and mnemonics. This was supported by a mixture of high- and low-stakes retrieval practice that was often interleaved with different elements of learning. This has helped develop a classroom culture where understanding and recalling precise examples of social research or theories is the norm, and something to be proud of. It has enabled students to appreciate that 'knowing' is something worthwhile and important.

Dialectic

Many students find it tough to understand what a sociological approach means. We decided to embed the habit of sociological discussion and critique so that students would arrive at lessons expecting to have the opportunity to practise doing what a sociologist does: analysing social research, testing hypotheses, evaluating social theories and justifying their own thoughts. Strategies such as 'think-pair-share' have been explicitly embedded into the scheme of work. However, the trivium encouraged us to think carefully about the relationship between grammar and dialect, and so debates, discussion and analysis are often teacher-led, modelling the type of questions sociologists ask or building in more complex analysis or controversy. Next year, we plan to use a 'Sociologists, Stop!' sign to indicate that not all is well with a particular 'social fact' or argument, and to reinforce a style of thinking when it comes to exploring sociologically. The precision and assessment of students' exploration of grammar will also continue to be highlighted; merely recalling specific knowledge does not necessarily equate to accurate application. Over time, we have seen students' choice of language in their essays (exam or otherwise) begin to change from a descriptive, black-and-white approach to one that is more analytical and appreciative of different stances.

Homework has also become an important way to help students engage with the more unusual aspects of sociology. Students are expected to choose 'excellent sociologist' tasks on top of set homework to broaden their understanding and love of the subject. This has ranged from listening to TED Talks through to offering a feminist–Marxist critique of a recent blockbuster. This has started to encourage a wider classroom culture of exploration.

Rhetoric

Using the idea of rhetoric has been one of the most helpful planning tools. It naturally led to the important question: what can a 16-year-old do to get an A* and become an excellent sociologist in their own right? Our answer was that they could co-construct their own piece of social research, conduct it, present it formally, accept critiques of it from others, and make a considered offering to the world of 'social facts'. This has included submitting a spoken presentation and a polished (redrafted) written research report in the style of a formal dissertation. Interestingly, students indicated this was their favourite part of the course. Using the notion of rhetoric and 'planning backwards' has helped raise the bar: our sociology curriculum is incredibly rigorous.

There are still many improvements to make; striving for mastery inevitably leads to an incredibly challenging curriculum. Ensuring that less able students can keep up requires careful scaffolding. Using the trivium as a framework can also be tricky: getting the balance right between the three aspects also requires careful planning, and knowing how to support students (is it the grammar or the dialect they aren't getting?) remains nuanced and unpredictable. However, the trivium has encouraged a culture of mastery, and it has been helpful as a planning tool.

Becky Hulme, Head of History

During a meeting with Martin Robinson earlier in the year, I had a personal revelation about the way history is delivered in my department. As I am now entering my eighth year of teaching and spend most of my time writing, updating and reviewing what are probably best described as quite rigid schemes of work, discussions inspired by the ideas of the trivium are welcome. We discussed the fact that I was grappling with the most effective method of delivering history (covering prehistory to modern history) in a given timescale to a mixed-ability group with a large disparity in prior achievement. The response was 'just teach'. We had a reflective conversation about what this really meant to the history discipline, and how I could underpin some of the chronology at Key Stage 3. It has reinforced the need for us to focus on chronology and provide students with a sense of period. We jump back and forwards in time to ensure history learning opportunities at Key Stage 3 are exploited, to expose students to the grammar they will need at GCSE.

Since joining Highbury Grove and leading the history department, my priority has been to create a learning experience that provides a balance between cultural capital and engaging students with history they can relate to. For example, we no longer teach a typical textbook response to World War II. Instead we analyse and evaluate the role played by countries in the British Empire, such as India and the West Indies, allowing students to act as historians and test their hypotheses through a documentary-style film. Therefore, the trivium has reinforced my view that grammar and dialectic are almost juxtaposed in history teaching and, with the right selection of key content, students are able to analyse, deduce, debate and synthesize historical enquiries – as is evident from the excellent documentary materials produced by our Year 9 students.

Working with the trivium while creating a local-history-based controlled assessment around the development of Sadler's Wells and Islington over the past ten months has encouraged me to take risks in how we teach history at Highbury Grove. Rather than differentiate original source material I gathered, with a colleague, from the local archives, we have used undifferentiated materials to drive challenge in lessons. For example, Year 10 history students were given a chapter to read each lesson followed by an additional chapter for homework. Initial concerns over what seemed our high expectations were quashed when one reluctant reader asked me politely, 'When can I have the next chapter?' Needless to say, I was overjoyed. The text, Dennis Arundell's *The Story of Sadler's Wells* contains some language and 18th/19th-century concepts that are unfamiliar to many of our students, yet using the piece in its original form strengthened the resilience of many students, providing both the grammar and oratory of rhetoric. The trivium has taught us that we should dedicate more time to facilitate challenging literacy lower down the school, providing an environment and framework where students feel confident in engaging and scrutinizing what they read. This is, of course, what we need every history learner at A level to do well.

Ruth Ramsden-Karelse, English teacher

The Trivium in Practice: Paperclip

We formed Paperclip, an equality and diversity discussion group, after two Year 10 students approached me in the corridor and said they felt the school needed a space where they could discuss issues that were important to them. Since its formation, Paperclip's focus has expanded and meandered: topics we've discussed include feminism, sexual identity, homophobia, gender identity, transphobia, body image, media pressure, racism, discrimination, the police, religion, patriarchy, gender roles, drag queens, prisons, gun control, political systems, animal rights and mental health. We currently have 15 regularly attending members; there are about 25 students at our biggest meetings. I believe that the work we do in Paperclip supports the students' growth into what Robinson calls philosopher kids with 'the confidence to [...] cultivate doubt – sometimes anger – and a desire to add to or change. [...] Importantly, an ability to take part in the great conversation and make a contribution towards our common life' (Robinson, 2013: 218). Over the course of the year, I've noticed a dramatic change in the way the students interact, listen, ask questions, and show confidence in disagreeing with – or sticking up for – others and themselves.

Our way of working, which from the outset has been student-led and exploratory, has developed organically to incorporate the three ways of the trivium: knowing, questioning and communicating. At the end of every meeting, we decide on our next area of focus and on which members of the group will lead us into this area. The following week, these students bring a stimulus – a story, article or video clip – and talk it through with the rest of us, thus facilitating the grammar component of our session. The dialectic – the discussion, questioning and debate of this new information – follows, and comprises the majority of each meeting. The students lead and manage all discussions, and their progress in this respect has been amazing to witness. Our learning usually resembles Robinson's model of the teacher as 'guide on the side' rather than 'sage on the stage', although we sometimes invite other teachers to run seminars with us, sharing their personal interests and expertise.

After meeting regularly for three months, the students in Paperclip decided that they wanted our meetings to have a more direct impact on life at our school. They subsequently invited our head teacher to one of our meetings and spoke to him with eloquence, passion and maturity about issues that were important to them. This experience highlighted Paperclip's realization of the importance of following through from grammar and dialectic to rhetoric, which is the final product of our sessions: the eloquent expression of the learning which has taken place through our discussion, questioning and debate. We have recently been working on developing and sharing this expression – for example, through our school newspaper and in assemblies.

Through Paperclip, we're attempting to achieve an education in morality. Of course, schools don't have a monopoly on values, but we are working on the premise of Socrates' claim, referenced by Robinson, that virtue is based on knowledge, and that all of society plays a role in imparting knowledge to the young. In Paperclip, students work together – exploring, questioning, achieving and expressing their opinion – to gain personal, experiential knowledge which is developing both their skills in these areas and their desire to seek improvement in all they see and do. These skills will help them to, as Robinson puts it, 'collaborate in order to restore, conserve and remake the world as [they see] fit' (Robinson, 2013: 170).

Sukhi Dhillon, Head of Maths

The Trivium in Maths Lessons

In my discussions with Martin, we explored the structure of typical maths lessons and the idea that they follow a trivium structure in many respects: knowledge input, exploration, problem-solving and discussion and, finally, the presentation of solutions. Our task is to draw this out and to make it more explicit. The first task is to check each unit of work for the basic mathematical skills required in order for students to be able to access the work successfully.

For example, when teaching algebraic fractions to Year 10, the grammar component is expressed as the core knowledge required: the basics of fractions and algebra and the key numeracy skills – adding, subtracting, multiplying and dividing with numbers. It's helpful to look at the roots of fractions and the roots of algebra and then to build up the ideas. Rather than making assumptions about what students already know, knowledge has to be continually revisited as many students have moved up without a secure understanding of the basics required for more advanced work.

The outcomes for a unit of work can then include opportunities where dialectic and rhetoric come into play. Students practise skills and increase their fluency; they engage in problem-solving and reasoning activities, individually and collaboratively. As their mastery grows, they learn to use the language of maths to explain their work, and then undertake assessments and mini-presentations of their work.

We're currently working on our assignments in maths so that we include sensible, practical opportunities for rhetoric: spontaneous chances for students to stand up by the board, explaining their solutions, and set-piece, pre-planned occasions to give a more extended exposition of key ideas, taking it in turns.

Next, we need to have a way of checking on our progress – a kind of audit tool, with different levels to aspire to. We've done some initial work with Martin on this, but it's at an early stage. Essentially, we think it would be useful to define some milestones along our path towards becoming the trivium school we envision. What might a basic level look like, where grammar, dialectic and rhetoric are happening regularly in the educational experience of every student? What might an advanced level look like, where the 'philosopher kids' concept is starting to sound like a description of our actual students, not just the ones we dream of improving? Perhaps this is a framework we could develop in conjunction with other schools as more schools embark on the same journey.

I'd like to conclude by thanking Martin Robinson for his significant contribution to our progress at Highbury Grove. Without *Trivium 21c,* we would probably be grappling with the same basic problems but we wouldn't have had the inspiration, the tools or the language to express the scale of our ambitions and the means of achieving them in the way we have. We're just at the start of what promises to be a fabulous journey. We're on a mission – *per ardua ad astra.*

References

Highbury Grove School (n.d.) 'The Highbury Grove School Framework for Teaching and Learning.' Available at: http://www.highburygrove.islington.sch.uk/curriculum/teaching-learning/framework-for-teaching-learning/.

Robinson, Martin (2013) *Trivium 21c: Preparing Young People for the Future with Lessons from the Past.* Carmarthen: Independent Thinking Press.

Chapter 3

The Trivium at Turton

Sam Gorse

Sam Gorse has been a teacher since 1993. She has been a pastoral lead, deputy head, and is now in her second year of headship at Turton School in Bolton. Turton is a large, thriving, 11–18 community school, on a thoughtful journey of continual improvement towards providing a better education for its students.

Sam is an idealist and a visionary in education. She believes that great teaching cultures and the importance of relationships are quite simply the means to a better education for all. For her, Trivium 21c is how we hold progressive and traditional methods in creative tension, without ever having to search for a compromise.

The work being done on the trivium at Turton shines out through this chapter, and also provides an interesting perspective on the subject from a school that Ofsted deemed Requires Improvement. During their first year of developing the trivium, an Ofsted inspection was announced. Read on to see how they got on.

Our Ofsted inspection in 2013 again raised the debate between tradition and progress. Ofsted's claim was that we were doing half the job perfectly – ethos, pastoral care, safeguarding, character education – but the other half – rigour and challenge in teaching – needed some work.

Let's put aside, for now, the fact that seeing education in two halves misses the point, and instead reflect on the possibility that perhaps the inspectors, like us, struggle to find the perfect balance between tradition and progress.

Turton is a progressive school: we are relentless in our focus to keep education moving forward, relevant and up to date for our young people. Our aim is to fully prepare students for their futures, both personally and academically. As such, we constantly challenge our thinking, searching for a balance between caring for and nurturing students, developing good character, and high academic achievement (as measured through GCSE outcomes).

It works much of the time in many areas, but we still have an underlying feeling that we haven't quite 'cracked the nut'.

After visiting Alexander McQueen's exhibition at the V&A, I had a moment of clarity thanks to one of his quotes: 'You've got to know the rules to break them. That's what I'm here for, to demolish the rules but keep the tradition.' I began to think that for some staff, the focus on being progressive – breaking tradition, thinking creatively – meant that they lost their foundation and were unable to see how modern thinking builds on the best of all that has previously been thought or said. I had led staff into a new, now deeply embedded, ethos, where teaching methods leaned largely towards dialectic and rhetoric styles, but hadn't realized that in so doing some staff misinterpreted this as an alternative to, rather than a strengthening of, traditional teaching methods and the rigour of knowledge and accuracy.

Tradition is unchanging, while progression requires change – thus the two are inherently opposing. This was the conflict raised by the visit of a very traditional inspection team. Some teachers, in embracing progress and searching for a meaningful education that develops good character and skills for life, had discarded tradition and all its benefits.

We needed to revisit the debate and look again at how we stay progressive but at the same time build more solid foundations in tradition: that is, use tradition as a base from which we can push forward the frontiers of understanding.

Our current journey began with a meaningful coincidence, a universal/cosmic force that some call 'fate'. During my first term as Head and my twelfth year at the school I set out an ambition: for the school to transform its teaching. The initial quest was how to maintain our ethos, hold true to our values and principles, provide the best possible education for our students and their futures, and achieve academic results as measured by government targets without 'gaming the system' or 'hothousing'. In short, how could we elicit the best of traditional and progressive methods?

During this time I set up a leadership book club. We began by reading *Trivium 21c* by Martin Robinson (Robinson, 2013). The book was drawn to our attention in Tom Sherrington's blog (Sherrington, 2014). We had no idea, prior to reading it, how synchronistic this would be. The leadership team was so inspired by *Trivium 21c* that we ordered further copies and began encouraging other staff to also read the book.

Conversations and debates about trivium infiltrated all our professional discussions and meetings. The concepts and philosophies began to spread like a rash: an energy and optimism was growing, and the feeling that we were beginning to find a way of transforming teaching so that it fitted perfectly with our values and principles – the type of transformation that had eluded us previously.

Subsequently working with Martin enabled us to find the language and professional conversations that would take us on a journey. With so many changes ahead, such as those coming through Ofqual to reform GCSEs, we felt it was more important than ever to ensure that our purpose was clear, that staff and students felt confident that education at Turton would serve its purpose in preparing students for their futures, and that any changes from the government fed into that purpose rather than hijacked it.

Working on the trivium has helped us to develop social capital. We are developing a school committed to building human relationships, committed to allowing people to come to know each other well and build trust among us. The purpose of this is to continue to improve the quality of education we provide. Talking to each other in a meaningful way about our subjects and about the purpose of education has strengthened and deepened our values and sense of community.

In his book, Martin claims that to be truly progressive you must have a firm foundation in grammar (Robinson, 2013: 73–75). We are a progressive school with a strong ethos, and within that we have departments that do an excellent job of combining the two. To move forward we needed to be sure that all departments, and indeed all individual teachers, had the skills to develop this harmony of tradition and progress within their areas to maximize learning, understanding and the development of good character throughout. We have all the elements at our disposal and some clear models of how the Trivium 21c is already working within schools. We are well placed, with Martin's support, to make this work and to provide a sustainable education for our students, with the added benefit of not being in or out of favour as political agendas change.

Our journey is well under way. Martin has spent time with many different departments, with a particular spotlight on maths. As English and maths rewrote their curriculums ready for September, Martin has inspired staff into meaningful and thoughtful discussions about teaching methodology, knowledge, understanding and the true place of dialectic and rhetoric in a student's learning.

A poignant debate began between Martin and one of our English teachers regarding student voice. This raised the notion that, while we pride ourselves on our students having the confidence, self-worth and articulation to express their thoughts and views freely, are we doing them a disservice if we don't first ensure that their opinions are well informed, thoughtful and supported by broad knowledge and understanding?

Nowhere is the debate between tradition and progress more obvious than in our maths department, where teaching and achievement have suffered from discord and a lack of purpose. Maths is a subject where a mastery curriculum is particularly key: it is one of the greatest cultural and intellectual achievements of humankind and is at the heart of modern working life. In order that students understand the importance and value of maths, pedagogy must draw out students' conceptual understanding of the subject. Lessons must be mathematically rich.

We have two distinct camps in maths: one of highly talented mathematicians with very traditional methods of teaching, and the other of less mathematically qualified teachers but with wonderfully progressive methods for engaging students. Neither camp could allow itself to develop the styles of the other and produce a truly effective combination of the best of both.

However, this was the department that took to Martin immediately: they embraced his ideas, they were enthused by the conversations he facilitated, and they loved exploring the grammar of maths.

The discussions and debate so far have cured the department of its anomie and brought everyone together on common ground. Maths teachers love talking about their subject, and so debates have centred on the grammar in maths to fire their passions and imaginations. This led to productive conversations around building a new curriculum, starting in Year 13, exploring what is required at this level, and working backwards to ensure that all learning along the way is embedded and timely.

We are now several months into our designs for a *Trivium 21c* education at Turton, and I would say that, while initially Martin seemed to be like Marmite, even those people who didn't take to the trivium at first are now being persuaded by the debate and the quality of the ideas put forward. The whole school feels energized, with some excellent work taking place on new curriculum proposals and developments in teaching.

Our intense discussions led to new ideas and plans, and what emerged was that this transformation could not be confined to a neat teaching 'box'. In order for the trivium to have a lasting impact and effect a cultural change, it had to infiltrate all our practices. Everything had to be adjusted in order to create an emerging culture for teaching at Turton. All systems had to focus on improving teaching.

Some of this is totemic, as we already have so much good stuff around. Some of it is proving to be more dramatic: we have crossed a Rubicon.

The most apposite and exciting of these changes is in appraisal. I say this because our previous appraisal process was completely unsatisfactory as it neither impacted on teaching quality nor aligned in any way with our ethos and climate. As a values-led school, we want accountability and development to work harmoniously side by side. Until now, we have rubber-stamped appraisals and refused to validate performance management. However, the trivium led us to a vision for appraisal and departmental review that would have improving teaching at its heart. Our new system activates pride, loyalty and a desire to improve among staff, requires little top-down monitoring, and assumes that everyone wants to improve.

Appraisal is organized into Turton Trivium Triads (we only like words beginning with T!). Each triad is a non-hierarchical group working collaboratively as critical friends to achieve mastery in the art and craft of teaching and learning. The flow of processes and activities between the triads forms a triangle of working CPD based on the notion that triangles form the strongest structure – because all three sides bear the load.

The triad is an ongoing teaching and learning group that focuses on the individual (CPD, appraisal, subject knowledge, strengths and improvements) and the triad team (collaboration, sharing ideas, embedding the trivium, professional dialectic and rhetorical discussions/debates) and student outcomes (being the best that we can be; inspiring students to be the best that they can be; constantly asking 'what impact am I having?').

Our previous appraisal amounted to a yearly one-to-one with a reviewer to set two or three targets for the year. So we started by signing off those targets and closing the old system. The triads represent a more open and cohesive form of professional development, where areas for improving teaching and impact are shared with triad members, the leader for your triad and your head of department to inform departmental reviews.

The first task of the triad was to agree on a definition for great teaching – thus starting with the end in mind. The next task was to engage in professional dialogue over time to establish three areas of focus for each person. The first is a negotiated shared focus that looks specifically at developing trivium teaching methods. The second is personal improvements to teaching, and the third is a focus on improving the student experience or school community.

The triad then set about getting to know each other as practitioners. It is up to them how they do this, but obvious examples are learning walks, drop-in observations, filming aspects of each other's lessons to be analysed by the group, looking at students' books, etc. They work together on planning, and reflect on how the planning impacts on students' learning.

Our October INSET day is dedicated time to review the process as a whole school, then we continue to work together in triads. It is an opportunity to share the journey so far, and its impact, with triad leaders. Each member of the leadership team then supports the review and progress of several triads.

As departmental reviews come around, improvement foci will be discussed with their head of department, who can then also engage in assessing progress and impact. This will then inform the department review process.

We had already removed judgement grades from our lesson observations, but this must be done more emphatically now. As we move away from levelling students in Key Stage 3 and grading everything a student does in Key Stage 4, we also move away from grading teachers' teaching. If we assume that everyone can improve, then grades are a distraction.

At the end of the year, each triad will evidence improvements over time and the impact on students' learning and progress.

Martin has helped us to speed up the process of infusing our vision for teaching. During his time here he worked with every department, ensuring he spoke to each teacher to enable them to understand and access the ideas and principles in our vision. Martin represented excellent value for money in this sense, because over a very short space of time he had had some impact on everyone. This worked alongside me talking to staff at every meeting and whole-school opportunity to spread the word.

Tim Brighouse has a model for implementing change which contains the following elements: vision + skills + incentive + resources + action plan. I am well aware that if 'vision' is the missing element in a culture change, or the vision isn't clear and shared by all, then anything that is put in place will lead to confusion.

People needed to understand the trivium: they needed to understand the thinking and ideas within it, and they needed to understand our current position as a school. Significantly, they needed to believe that I work on the assumption that everyone wants to improve and that improving teaching is our collective aim.

Adding to that, the leadership team began looking at high-impact, low-effort ideas to ensure that we brought all staff into the philosophies, conversations and debates. We wanted the trivium to be the focus of our future culture for teaching, but we did not want to force prescriptive systems and procedures on everyone – that is not our ethos. We believe that the values and principles, the philosophies and cultures are common to us all, but the methodology, curriculum and pedagogy must be in some way unique to each department and each individual.

We wanted people to feel empowered by their own thinking and inspired by others' ideas and successes. At the same time, we wanted people to continually embed and develop trivium teaching methods and ideologies.

A most effective high-impact, low-effort idea is the use of our briefing time. This also has the advantage of providing fuel for the triads, adding ideas, information and successes to the work within triad groups. Briefing time works by using the time as a conversation starter for the week. A thought-provoking question or idea is emailed to staff beforehand, for example:

> Starting with the grammar, at what point do we introduce dialectic and rhetoric for each topic?

What is the impact of grammar, dialectic and rhetoric on character education?

Staff are invited to join the briefing early for coffee and discussion, and as the formal briefing starts one or two people will share their thoughts and ideas on how the trivium is infiltrating their practice. This may then form the basis for next week's discussion, giving some continuity to the weekly discussions.

Our head of geography gave a particularly inspiring two-minute talk on his work on the trivium in geography. This was followed by an email to staff ahead of the next briefing:

Thanks to Clive for sharing his thoughts on life after levels and embedding the trivium into geography. He made a beautiful, thought-provoking analogy to a mountain top, evoking not only references to Martin Luther King but also sparking some interesting points for discussion. Clive's reference to the mountain top and how you might not always understand everything you see first time round, but that the view is nonetheless still amazing, made me think. He alluded to the idea that giving Year 7 the view from the top, so to speak, and asking staff to keep in mind the end goal of what makes the 'master geographer' is how we build learning power and desire within our students. The trivium is about breadth and depth, and the view from the mountain top is certainly expansive. It raises many questions for us as a teaching team. In order to keep the dialectic going – and continuing on from Clive's observations – we would like to discuss the following questions in next Monday's briefing:

- How soon should students be shown the view from the top?
- How do we promote the awe and wonder that the view should inspire?

- How do we provide breadth without it being at the expense of depth?

This email was sent to staff by Carole Baily, assistant head teacher (teaching and learning), and gives an idea of the momentum that this ten-minute weekly dialogue has gained over a term, with Carole's emails being the engine that keeps it moving forward.

Of course, our trivium journey began as we were redesigning curriculums for 'life after levels' and new GCSEs. My messages needed to be clear about how the trivium would enhance and inform our current work, give it meaning and direction (and certainly not just be 'something else to do'!).

It's very easy to get caught in the trap of replacing national curriculum levels with equally banal categories such as emerging, developing, securing, mastery, especially as there are many examples of 'good practice' being pushed our way. But instead of replacing national curriculum levels with new criteria-led assessments, I insisted that we use the trivium to refocus on what children need to learn at each stage and use a mixture of techniques to establish whether something has been learned (or not yet) at each stage. The removal of levels is an opportunity to move away from the notion that we need to categorize children, and instead focus on teaching our subjects and the skills and knowledge we want children to learn.

Every teacher should know what excellence looks like in their subject and be able to clearly define this for their students. Teachers should be clear about the depth and rigour of the answers they expect, and measure progress using students' spoken and written work.

A great example of this is in a video I saw which demonstrated the Steiner education method. It shows a boy being interviewed about his work. When asked about the progress he was making, the boy opens his book and shows the interviewer a map of the UK he has produced. The boy tells the interviewer that he knows he is making good progress because this is the best map of the UK he has ever drawn.

My vision is to intervolve care, support and guidance – and the Turton ethos – with transformational teaching that develops character and lifelong learning. Never again will Ofsted accuse us of only excelling in half the job!

This is being done through combining the tradition of knowledge and grammar with progressive methods using dialectic and rhetoric, all in a culture of excellence, compassion, creativity and thoughtful hard work.

My children were educated in a local comprehensive school during a time when the focus on GCSE outcomes was all that seemed to matter. They were taught to pass exams and 'fit into' school expectations. They did the first reasonably well, in varying degrees, and the second reasonably badly, in varying degrees. Now in their early twenties, teachers and lawyers themselves, they remember little of what they were taught at school.

I want the students at Turton to learn – and to love learning. I want them to reflect on their education in later life and, rather than counting their A*–C passes, I want them to feel that their five or seven years here were worthwhile because they learned useful and interesting stuff that enhanced their lives. Most importantly, I want them to develop a love of learning that will stay with them.

We are on a journey, with the trivium as our guide. Some practical, geographical changes have helped to create energy and drive, and have brought people together in new groups and with new dialogues. We call these changes 'zoning' because we have changed the location of departments and the use of spaces around the school site to create zones where, for example, different groups of subjects work together. Some of this is about our best teachers and departments influencing others, and some of it is about opening doors between subjects, but largely it is about expanding collegiality, so that it impacts on improving teaching and student outcomes.

Zoning required an enormous community effort initially, with site staff and support staff working tirelessly over the summer to prepare spaces for the new year. Without the cooperation and support of support staff, these changes would have been either impossible or involved expensive contractors.

The zones are specific to our unique requirements: for example, the dining room has been expanded to create opportunities for character development by the design of a shared space with drama. All student support facilities are now located in the true centre, or geographical heart, of the site, with all zones emanating from there. English and modern foreign languages share a zone to enable our strongest teachers to influence others. They share coffee mornings, they share grammar ideas and they develop mutual planning.

Zoning encourages breadth across subject boundaries. Subjects with shared grammar can work together. Some subjects are grouped on the basis that the dialectic of a topic would require teachers to bring in branches of knowledge from other subjects in order to help students reason and understand issues or concepts: for example, the conflict unit in geography requires grammar from history and politics.

The notorious 'Hannah's sweets' problem from the 2015 Edexcel Maths GCSE paper raised the argument that students struggle to solve complex problems because they're not taught to problem-solve by combining several concepts in maths. Instead, everything is taught discretely, by topic and by subject.

Students do like to learn things in boxes: however, our job is to stick the boxes together and open doors between them – this is the aim of our zoning. Zoning will connect the learning experience, with a focus on creativity, sharing and the importance of developing learning for life.

During the summer term, I interviewed several colleagues for an internal post. They were asked for their thoughts on the trivium, and one woman's response stuck in my mind. She claimed that, for the first time since her teacher training, she was having conversations (and not just in meetings, but at lunchtime and socially) about the purpose of education, and that this had reignited her passion for teaching and given her a feeling of fulfilment that she had lost through consecutive government agendas.

The trivium is broadening our collective understanding of the purpose of education at Turton, bringing together the traditionalists and the progressives in a vision that has at its centre the moral aspects of education.

Ultimately our purpose is reflected in this quote from Archbishop Desmond Tutu, 'It is our moral obligation to give every child the very best education possible.' Archbishop Desmond Tutu (Tutu and Van Roekel, 2010).

The trick is figuring out how to do this, however, and what 'the best education' looks like. The trivium represents a culture shift in teaching at Turton: as such, everything related to teaching must shift into that culture. Some of this is about the leadership of the school creating the conditions for the shift, and some of it is about the teachers and support staff committing to continual improvement; but most significantly it is about committing to the long view, where impact is expected over time, rather than settling for quick fixes that are unsustainable.

In May 2015 Ofsted came back. They acknowledged the improvements we had made to our teaching, and (having read *Trivium 21c* themselves) agreed to all our work on the trivium and its early impact on our practice, recognizing that we are on a journey to find that perfect balance and make teaching at Turton truly great.

At each stage along the way I remind myself of a quote from *The Best Exotic Marigold Hotel*: 'Everything will be alright in the end, so if it's not alright, it's not yet the end.' I know that this journey will take us towards improving the quality of what we provide, and that along the way it will allow everyone at Turton to work together in a purposeful and meaningful way that is true to our values and principles.

References

Robinson, Martin (2013) *Trivium 21c: Preparing Young People for the Future with Lessons from the Past.* Carmarthen: Independent Thinking Press.

Sherrington, Tom (2014) 'Trivium 21st C: Could this be the answer?' *Headguruteacher* [blog] (17 January). Available at: http://headguruteacher.com/2014/01/17/trivium-21st-c-could-this-be-the-answer/.

Tutu, Desmond and Van Roekel, Dennis (2010) 'Facing the Future: Global Education at the Crossroads', *The Huffington Post* (21 June). Available at: www.huffingtonpost.com/desmond-tutu/facing-the-future-global_b_544449.html.

Chapter 4

The Trivium as a Prism

Nick Wells

Swindon Academy was the first all-through academy in the UK, educating children from the age of 2 through to 19. Nick is very proud to be the Vice Principal responsible for Teaching and Learning in the secondary phase. The staff at Swindon Academy make no secret of their ambition to strive for excellence in every aspect of school life, and for all children. They aim high, dream big and reach far. They treat children as individuals, and are strongly committed to equality of opportunity, wanting all children to succeed both academically and socially, so that they will be well prepared for adult life in a changing society.

On reading *Trivium 21c*, Nick and his team were struck by the way it offered them a way of rethinking what they had begun in moving the school forward. This chapter explores that process.

Prism: A glass or other transparent object in the form of a prism, especially one that is triangular with refracting surfaces at an acute angle with each other and that separates white light into a spectrum of colours.

I'd like to begin our chapter by introducing you to three students whose tales, although fictionalized, are based on real students from our academy. Their experiences illuminate a lot of the thinking behind the journey which the academy has been on over the past three years. We'll call them Sam, Ellie and Will. Their stories cast a spotlight on our past, but also point towards the reasons we now do things differently.

The first of these students, Ellie, made masses of progress during her two years in our sixth form. The transformation in the quality of her essay-writing was a delight to observe. At the start of Year 12 she didn't have a full grasp of what an essay was. She had been able to produce coursework across a range of subjects at GCSE level, but she had all manner of confused notions about literary terminology, and wouldn't have believed for one second that she'd be able to quote Shakespeare to you. Despite being pleased that Ellie came out of her closed-book exam buzzing because she'd written 12 pages and carried out some excellent analysis of the quotations she'd committed to memory, I couldn't help but think she'd have been even better off if she'd arrived at the start of Year 12 being able to do much of this already – having had an education which had exposed her to the best that has been thought and said.

Sam, like a number of our Year 11 students, had experienced some tragic events at home, both before and during his GCSE years. Though I believe his subsequent low attendance impacted on his progress during Key Stage 3, Sam had also learned a whole myriad of work avoidance strategies – he was the king of the oblique question. At various points in his education, he had been allowed to opt out. By allowing him to develop these strategies, we accepted that Sam was less likely to do well in his GCSEs. Sam did get his 'five Cs', but could have achieved Bs and As.

Will arrived in Year 7 having been fairly successful in his Year 6 SATS, though not as successful as some of his peers. However, he was driven and motivated. He was a vociferous reader of both fiction and non-fiction across a wide range of subject areas, he thought deeply without the need for much prompting, and he provoked thought in others. He left sixth form with a clutch of top grades. However, he failed to be offered a place at Cambridge, partly as a result of the more limited range of wider opportunities which he'd been offered or taken up.

In order to avoid students like Sam developing poor learning habits and students like Ellie arriving in Year 12 without the academic foundations to fly from the outset, and to ensure students like Will have access to the best opportunity to secure places on top university courses, we began to move towards a model of curriculum design, planning and teaching that is informed by our reading and research. We had started to implement what we've described as a mastery curriculum, having been inspired by the work of Bruno Reddy and others at King Solomon Academy. We drew on the teaching model developed by Shaun Allison at Durrington High School in Sussex. We also began to implement a number of the principles found in *Teach Like A Champion* by Doug Lemov (2010).

Around the same time, our Principal, Ruth Robinson, and I came across Martin's first book, *Trivium 21c* (Robinson, 2013) via Tom Sherrington's blog. Separately, we had both read Tom's blog (Sherrington, 2014) and suspected that Martin's thinking would tie in well with our academy's journey of improvement. However, we'd also both left reading the book until the end of the autumn term of 2014. Ruth referred to it during a conversation about teaching, asking me if I'd read it already. We decided at that point that we'd both add it to our Christmas lists that year.

As I read it, in the post-Christmas haze which can be the result of having overly excitable children who can't get back to sleep after 5am, I was fascinated by the history which Martin narrates and critiques. I had read very little about educational history and was relatively ignorant of the debates that have taken place about the purposes of education. Towards the end of the book, when Martin discusses how the trivium might be implemented in a contemporary setting, I began to see that it might be used as a prism to separate, or refract, our own school improvement process into its constituent parts. Observing the aspects of our development in this new light might enable us to re-evaluate our work so far, in order to enhance it for the benefit of our teachers and students. In particular, it struck me that, if we were to structure our mastery curriculum in a manner that linked it to the trivium, then we would see our students fly even higher than they have done in the past – not just in terms of their exam results, but also in terms of their understanding of, and ability to contribute to, the world around them.

To kick-start this process, I attempted to take a dialectic approach by establishing a set of questions to ask ourselves to review our academy in the light of the trivium. These swiftly morphed from questions into implications linked to the three elements of the trivium. Many of these, initially, were quite generic. As I continued to think, they became more specific to our academy's structures and processes. We discussed these implications with other senior leaders and, subsequently, with our curriculum leaders, in the manner below.

Grammar Implications

In his book, Martin traces the history of grammar from its beginnings as the study of Greek and then Latin and Hebrew, on to its evolution into a deep study of literature, and ending up with its later meaning of the study of the foundational aspects of a culture. However, in *Trivium 21c,* Martin takes 'grammar' to mean the knowledge relevant to a specific subject domain. He argues that, 'In order to be critical and creative, kids need to know stuff, to have a good grasp of the basics, the grammar of a topic' (Robinson, 2013: 217).

Martin argues, 'The grammarian will tell it like it is, either by agreed practice or imposed rules' (Robinson, 2013: 40). They are focused on facts and the way things are supposed to be done. As Martin states, there is a finite amount of time in a school day, so schools need to consider whether they are exposing their students to a broad and rich curriculum, as Anthony Seldon puts it, 'those aspects that are proven by time to be enduring rather than the ephemeral' (quoted in Robinson, 2013: 227).

We had already reviewed our curriculum for Year 7. However, the first implication of the trivium was that our faculties needed to continue to clearly define the factual and procedural knowledge which they had to teach, and which they wanted students to retain in order to be successful into Years 8, 9 and beyond. This process linked to both our mastery curriculum and our teaching and learning model in terms of providing appropriate challenge. In order to achieve this, we generated a set of questions to review what had been done so far with Year 7 and what needed to be done in Years 8 and 9. Questions included 'How have you defined the knowledge which you want students to retain from Year 7, and how will you assess this in Year 8?' and 'Have enough opportunities been built in for students to apply the knowledge they have gained in speech, writing, through problem-solving, performance or developing products?' You can probably see the influence of the trivium here.

Our secondary head teacher and I then met with each of our curriculum leaders to discuss these questions, and we held a curriculum leaders' planning day, during which they reviewed each other's curriculum models, probing, questioning and advising each other.

We also realized that implementing a richer curriculum would mean that we needed to enable staff to further develop their subject knowledge so that they could fully support and stretch even more children to learn. In order to achieve this, we asked each curriculum leader to set up a self-review process whereby teachers would audit their subject knowledge against each module they were going to be teaching. Stronger staff would provide training and/or support for teachers who needed further guidance. Where there was a need for an area to be developed across a faculty, we would know that we needed to seek external support. This work will continue into the coming academic year and, given the changes to the curriculum nationally, it is highly likely to be ongoing.

In line with our Teaching and Learning model, we identified that we need to hone our great teaching techniques to pass on new knowledge, explain new concepts clearly and precisely, and model new procedures to our students. We also need to continue tightening up on consistency and providing bespoke training for staff, focusing on the core aspects of our Teaching and Learning model: Challenge, Explanations, Modelling, Questioning and Feedback (linked to *Teach Like a Champion:* Lemov, 2010). So as to achieve this, we have – for the past two years – held four of our training days together at the start of the academic year. This has enabled us to focus on specific aspects of teaching which we want to be in place from the beginning of the year when teachers and students are at their freshest. We then continue to develop these through our coaching process. All of our teachers have a coach who works with them either once a week or fortnightly. We also run monthly two-hour training slots to build on the work done in September. Finally, we have produced an electronic Teaching and Learning Handbook which includes video footage of the strategies and techniques that feature in our teaching model. In terms of our monitoring procedures, we have placed a firm emphasis on curriculum leaders working alongside senior leaders to take responsibility for the quality of teaching within their faculties.

In addition to this, in terms of grammar, we need to make even better use of assessment (formatively in class and formally in exams) to check that students have retained knowledge, and take action where they have not. If students are to be able to successfully move effectively towards dialectic and rhetoric, their knowledge needs to be secure. This year we are trialling the use of online multiple-choice quizzes to help teachers provide immediate feedback to students relating to their retention of knowledge. Later in the year, we will also provide our curriculum leaders with training on producing more reliable assessment models.

We need to ensure that our students have, at their fingertips, effective strategies to memorize new material and retain and recall old material. We will encourage this through the development of our revision guides, our tutor programme, and in-class support from teachers. Finally, we need to provide our students with great opportunities to practise important procedures so that they become automatic. This will be achieved through our curriculum planning and delivery in the classroom.

Dialectic Implications

In *Trivium 21c* Martin establishes that dialectic consists of the questioning of principles and abstract ideas using reasoning, logic and debate. To aid understanding, he characterizes three types of dialectician.

- Socratic dialecticians argue for argument's sake. They 'will ask about it until it is no longer'.
- Platonic dialecticians 'will discuss it until "ultimate truth" is revealed'.
- Aristotelian dialecticians will seek to uncover all of the possible 'truths' and can accept that more than one position or 'truth' is possible (Robinson, 2013: 40).

In order to be more successful here, as an academy we need to define when – in each subject, in each unit and in each key stage across our school – we want our students to be ready for debate, questioning and philosophizing. In order to do this effectively, teachers and subsequently students need domain-related knowledge as well as knowledge of the processes and conventions used in philosophical/logical debate. This will be achieved through the review of our mastery curriculum, through the spoken language elements in our English teaching, and through the tutorial programme. However, we also need to more clearly define the practices which enable this stage of the learning process to occur effectively in our classrooms and learning environments. We will do this through staff training as well as through our handbook.

Rhetoric Implications

Rhetoric is defined by Martin as communicating and expressing learning. This can be in written or spoken form or in the form of a performance – the form will suit the subject the student is focusing on. Rhetoricians seek to communicate knowledge, choosing and arranging words well, understanding and manipulating others' emotions, with great culture, sensitivity, humour and memory.

To improve our provision here, we need to ensure that tasks stretch all our students and prepare students for the next stage in their lives. Next year, we will be working a lot on the quality of our questioning, as well as the quality of modelling we carry out for our students to demonstrate to them that we expect them to aim for – and be able to achieve – excellence.

We also need to design homework tasks at this stage which are more open-ended. To achieve this, we have worked with curriculum leaders on a model that will help them monitor the quality of homework being set by teachers.

The Movement from Dependence to Independence

Towards the end of the book, Martin explains how the trivium can also be used to teach students to move from dependence to independence. He suggests that we move from the directive phase, through the guided phase and on to a phase he calls 'receptive–exploratory' (Robinson, 2013: 226). In the directed phase we focus on the grammar, or what David Didau calls the 'field' in his teaching sequence for developing independence (Didau, 2014: 22). We also set the context for improvement and the 'big picture'. At this stage there is likely to be plenty of teacher explanation and modelling. Doug Lemov calls this the 'I' stage. During guided discovery, leadership is shared by the teacher and student. This stage is likely to feature modelling, shared construction or deconstruction of new models as well as deliberate, possibly supported, practice. This is where students will do much of their questioning (dialectic) of both the grammar and the models. Lemov calls this stage 'We'. During the receptive–exploratory phase, ownership moves away from the teacher and increasingly to the student. Then students apply their knowledge of content and the models they have seen in creation or performance. This is the rhetoric stage of the process, which Didau (2014: 47) calls independent construction and Lemov calls 'You' (see Robinson, 2013: 226).

At our academy, we don't prescribe a specific model of lesson, in that we don't have a three-part lesson or a five-part lesson or an eight-part lesson. We don't have a lesson sequence which we expect in every lesson. We don't expect teachers to have any number of mini-plenaries just because they've been told to, and we don't limit the amount of teacher talk to 5 minutes out of every 65 minutes. This is because we believe that the lesson is not necessarily the best unit of learning – and therefore not the best starting point for planning.

Having said this, we do have a set of Swindon Academy expectations in terms of operating in the classroom. What was most exciting about the trivium for us was that it seemed to lend itself to an adaptation, or evolution, of our model of teaching. Our reading of the book led to the two following models. The first of these defines our curriculum design (see page 62). The second defines our teaching model (see page 63).

In terms of future developments, we will continue to focus on these three aspects of our curriculum and teaching model. We are also keen to explore the work which Tom Sherrington has begun with Martin in relation to building assignment outlines, ensuring students have opportunities to secure knowledge, develop their understanding and enhance their ability to apply their skills. We have begun to see already that this embedded, longer-term approach can pay dividends in terms of students' outcomes in examinations. More importantly, though, we are convinced that this will also enrich their lives.

<table>
<tr><td rowspan="2">We contribute to curriculum design
So that …
The knowledge, threshold concepts and performances, creations or products are established for every Scheme of Learning.</td><th>A Trivium Based Mastery Curriculum</th><th colspan="4">Objectives are manageable, measureable, made first and important</th></tr>
<tr><td>Know
Learning the knowledge relevant to subject domain. To be critical and creative students need to know relevant content.</td><td rowspan="3">Curriculum planning
■ Working together, using exam specifications and their subject knowledge, teams of teachers define threshold concepts and learning objectives which will be mapped into Schemes of Learning to help all students to achieve them.</td><td rowspan="3">Underlying beliefs
■ Teachers believe that virtually all students can learn all important academic knowledge to a level of excellence.</td><td rowspan="3">Teaching demonstrating high expectations
■ Teaching sets a high level of challenge.
■ Explanations, modelling, questioning, feedback and the classroom environment encourage and generate a high level of challenge.</td><td rowspan="3">Cycle of teaching and assessment
■ Learning is class paced rather than unit paced.
■ Whole class work is carried out initially – teaching the material.
■ A first formative test is carried out.
■ Learning alternatives/ correctives/therapies are used to ensure all students achieve a level of excellence.
■ Re-testing occurs.
■ Any additional steps are taken.
■ A summative test is used.</td></tr>
<tr><td rowspan="2">We have high expectations of our pupils
So that …
We plan for a high level of challenge, believing that virtually all students can learn contents and skills to a level of excellence.</td><td>Understand
Questioning of principles and abstract ideas using reasoning, logic and debate.</td></tr>
<tr><td>Be Able To
Communicating and expressing learning in written or spoken form or in the form of a performance or product.</td></tr>
</table>

Swindon Academy – Teaching the Trivium

Swindon Academy teachers: ENSURE STUDENTS BROADEN THEIR KNOWLEDGE:	Swindon Academy teachers: ENSURE STUDENTS DEEPEN THEIR UNDERSTANDING:	Swindon Academy teachers: ENSURE STUDENTS' WRITING, PERFORMANCES, DESIGNS AND CREATIONS ARE OF AN EXCELLENT STANDARD:
We plan, model, direct, make connections to what students know already. We direct and name the steps, expect students to make excellent notes and practice to achieve excellence in class and for homework. We question to check their knowledge and provide feedback to let them know how close to 100% they are. TLaC Strategies: No Opt Out, At Bats, Call and Response, Show Me, Right is Right, Format Matters, Name the Steps, Pepper.	We guide students to make new discoveries, expect them to give full answers and stretch their answers with further questions. We ask students how and why, give them wait time to think effectively, share students' answers to explore their effectiveness. We expect students to devise questions of their own and debate and explore complex concepts. TLaC Strategies: Plan for Error, Culture of Error, Excavate Error, Stretch It, Wait Time, Everybody Writes, Turn and Talk (Pair Share), Habits of Discussion, Art of the Sentence, Cold Call.	We coach students, challenge them and provide them with tutorials. We demand that they move towards professionalism, expecting them to write and speak fluently. We plan opportunities for self-reflection and improvement, opening up new questions. We increasingly expect independence, setting up open ended tasks and we assess their work to identify how they could produce something even better next time.

References

Didau, David (2014) *The Secret of Literacy*. Carmarthen: Independent Thinking Press.

Lemov, Doug (2010) *Teach Like a Champion: 49 Techniques That Put Students on the Path to College*. San Francisco, CA: Jossey-Bass.

Robinson, Martin (2013) *Trivium 21c: Preparing Young People for the Future with Lessons from the Past*. Carmarthen: Independent Thinking Press.

Sherrington, Tom (2014) 'Trivium 21st C: Could this be the answer?' *Headguruteacher* [blog] (17 January). Available at: http://headguruteacher.com/2014/01/17/trivium-21st-c-could-this-be-the-answer/.

Chapter 5

Enriching the Learning Experience

David Hall

Nigel Matthias, Nick Barnsley

Using the Trivium to Develop Curriculum and Assessment and Build Cultural Capital at Bay House School

Bay House School and Sixth Form is an 11–18 academy in Hampshire, serving a diverse and comprehensive catchment of pupils and students.

This chapter outlines the work that the senior leadership team has been doing within the school, using the principles of the trivium to enrich the curriculum and the learning experiences of pupils and students. In particular, the chapter describes the work that is being done to develop a more progressive curriculum and assessment approach from Year 7 through to Year 11. There is an exploration of how they have used the trivium to develop a new programme of study, centred on the history of philosophical ideas and thinking, to support and engage students, particularly those who want to complete the Extended Project Qualification (EPQ). Finally, the approach that the school is taking in promoting rhetoric through speech making in Year 7 is outlined.

The authors are David Hall (Associate Head Teacher), Nigel Matthias (Deputy Head Teacher) and Nick Barnsley (EPQ Lead and history teacher).

Introduction

Bay House School is a large 11–18 comprehensive school in Gosport, Hampshire, that converted to an academy in 2012. We serve a very broad catchment of pupils, drawing from relatively affluent areas as well as some of the more socioeconomically deprived areas of the town. Our school community is predominantly white British. We recognize the particular responsibilities that we have to such a population, and consequently are continually reflecting on the learning experiences that we are offering. In particular, are we confident that our curriculum is challenging and that we are providing our learners with new perspectives? Are we motivating our learners to be ambitious and to think in different ways? How successful are we at promoting and building the cultural capital of our youngsters?

As a converter academy we have had the opportunity to design our curriculum beyond that which is prescribed nationally. However, as is often the case, the realities of such 'freedoms' are never entirely straightforward. Indeed, being given such flexibility can appear overwhelming and teachers, living in a culture of high external accountability, are therefore more likely to retreat to the safety of a consistent framework. We were keen to support our subject leaders and other colleagues involved in curriculum design so that they could take advantage of our academy status and begin to explore in greater depth the more fundamental questions of what we want education at Bay House to be about.

First, we set about exploring five key strategic questions through our middle and senior leadership forums in the school:

1. What do we want our pupils to learn? How are we responding to the new national curriculum? Is this what we want?

2. What learning capacities do we want our pupils to develop so that their understanding of *how* they are learning grows? How are we ensuring that we are addressing these capacities (recognizing that some capacities can be generic but that many are developed in different ways through subjects)?

3. How confident are we that our assessment strategies are linked to the objectives and the learning activities? Are we confident that these are fit for purpose and that their impact is ensuring sustained progress for all?
4. How are we mapping the learning and progression of pupils from Year 7 to Year 11, dismantling the notion that GCSE learning has to start in Year 10?
5. How are we leading on the development of teaching and professional development to enable the above?

We have used these questions as a vehicle to express our core ethos: that is, a curriculum that progressively builds knowledge and skill from the beginning of a pupil's time with us, and that also fosters effective habits and attitudes to learning. In addition, we no longer want assessment to be the 'tail that wags the dog' through a continual diet of end-of-unit tests. Rather, we should be designing more sophisticated approaches that allow us to better understand what pupils can and can't do. This has become particularly pertinent since the reporting of national curriculum levels has ceased.

Through our engagement with the trivium principles, and with a number of our colleagues working directly with Martin, it is evident that our ethos and values are very strongly aligned. For example, a review of the five strategic questions above highlights grammar within the first question, dialectic within the second, and rhetoric within the third. In truth, all three strands of the trivium are interwoven throughout.

We are at the start of our journey in the development of trivium principles at Bay House, and we are all excited about where this will take us. We have identified some key areas that we are currently working on, and this chapter will discuss these in more detail.

The Trivium – Curriculum and Assessment

Our decision to shape a curriculum approach around progression from Year 7 to Year 11, in which we abandoned the notion of key stages, provided rich opportunities for our colleagues to engage in highly productive, albeit challenging, discussions. These have been centred on an examination of what we value as 'core' knowledge in our subjects, and what are the subject-specific learning habits that we want to foster and develop. Enabling this model of progression necessitated careful consideration of the 'starting point' within each subject discipline: that is, what are the threshold concepts or skills that pupils will need to master to fully engage and develop their understanding further? Our engagement with the trivium is supporting subject leaders as they wrestle with these fundamental questions and develop new schemes of learning, both for the short and the longer term.

Furthermore, the development of our new curriculum models, with their inherent exploration of what we want our learners to know and do (and when we want them to have done it) raised another critical question – how will we know that they have mastered and understood new knowledge or a new skill? Our introduction to the principles of the trivium was fortuitous: it was at a time when we were grappling with the deep-seated issues of the nature and purpose of assessment, set against a national backdrop of significant upheaval in education.

Like most secondary schools, Bay House School and Sixth Form greeted the Department for Education's decision to remove national curriculum levels with a combination of excitement and trepidation. Suddenly we were presented with an exciting opportunity to demonstrate that a reinvigorated system of assessment was possible – but sometimes it was difficult to see that we should be more excited than daunted at the prospect. It represented a clear chance to demonstrate the professionalism of the teaching profession. We recognized the need to devise a system that was precise, reliable and simple to understand for a wide audience.

However, we quickly became engaged in a rather internecine conflict between 'traditional' approaches and more 'progressive' methods of assessment. The introduction of the trivium helped us to see a third way: we did not have to choose the 'dialectician' in preference to the 'grammarian', the traditional ahead of the progressive, but instead we could devise methods of assessment that included elements of all these areas. We quickly formed a steering group, but much of our discussion mirrored an issue at the core of the trivium: the centuries-old debate about the balance between what and how much pupils should learn, how much time should be allocated to thinking and criticizing those ideas, and how much time should be left for the communication of these ideas. It was at this stage we began to ask whether the three ways of the trivium – knowing, questioning and communicating – could also underpin our approach to assessment. We were also attracted to one of the key trivium principles: the idea of a developing curriculum that responds to change as well as being rooted in an awareness of the importance of traditions.

There were, of course, practical considerations for us as school leaders. We agreed that, whatever day-to-day assessment we opted for, or created, pupils had to be tested against some form of benchmark during the course of each year. This was clear. We need to be able to demonstrate what our pupils have learned and what progress they are making, ensuring that they are on track to meet expectations, so that we can take action if individual pupils are falling behind.

We strongly believed, however, that our assessment methods should be the servant, not the master, of our curriculum. In other words, the accountability system should work with, not against, our main objective – which is to help our pupils to gain the skills and qualifications they need to succeed in future.

Overall, we agreed that any assessment system must allow us to have the following:

1. Clear conversations about who is making progress towards strong performance at GCSE (or equivalent) in each class/department (from the start of Year 7).
2. A clear overview of achievement that allows heads of department, heads of year, teachers and tutors to have an accurate idea of where the weaknesses are in their department (meetings can be specific).

3. Clear accountability for ensuring that gaps in pupils' knowledge are diagnosed, with appropriate intervention put into place in specific areas at the earliest possible opportunity.
4. Clear predictions about future performance from the start of Year 7, not just from Year 10. Our current system does not facilitate accurate forecasting of future performance. Our goal in changing our assessment system is, in essence, the same as that of *Trivium 21c* – to prepare young people for the future and to be assured that we are doing it effectively.

We quickly discovered, however, that whatever system we devised, the quality of classroom-based assessments was always going to determine the quality of the information we collected. One of the approaches we took with our middle leaders was to look critically at the sheer range of assessment practices and then evaluate their effectiveness. What quickly became evident was that the trivium model provided a very coherent structure for organizing our existing approaches.

Some curriculum leaders were more in favour of the 'grammar' forms of assessment: multiple-choice questions, tests of memory and the use of 'show me' personal whiteboards. Others favoured forms of assessment generally deemed more 'progressive': 'pair and share', deeper questioning and complex dialogue between teachers and pupils. The remaining strategies could be considered as forms of 'rhetoric': peer dialogue and assessment, essays and performances and mastery teaching. We also found ourselves challenged by the use of self and peer assessment and the relative 'dangers' of these forms of assessment. That is to say, that both self and peer assessment can be limited if pupils do not fully understand the success criteria against which assessment is being made. Without this, feedback through these approaches risks being shallow, tokenistic and is not meaningful. We had become quite comfortable with the day-to-day use of these techniques but our engagement with the trivium allowed us to engage with the importance of timing in peer assessment. The guiding principle of 'taste and judgement' – while controversial – was essential, as all too often a pupil's assumption that their opinion is inherently correct was not conducive to producing the collegiate classroom culture for which we were striving.

Whatever form of criteria or descriptor we devised, no matter how carefully constructed, inevitably led to the question of whether we would end up 'teaching to the test'. Michael Gove memorably declared that it was not problematic teaching to the examination per se, 'if the test is right', but as a school we were becoming increasingly uncomfortable with this idea (House of Commons, 2012). The trivium provided a degree of challenge that meant that our assessment system had to capture pupils' moments of joy and wonder, and their awareness of how to communicate knowledge and argument in a considered and thoughtful fashion. We did not want to create pupils who were simply experts at carefully constructing examination-friendly prose, but rather create an assessment system that allowed the experience and wonder of studying the subjects themselves to shine through.

So, what next? While our system remains a work in progress, we have shared our initial work on assessment with the head teachers of junior and infant schools in our cluster, and asked them this very question. Our cluster now has a shared excitement about embracing the opportunity to collaborate and create an information-rich method of assessing progress in a way that is much more valuable than a mere score or grade. We are now looking at how we can use the trivium principles to improve the way we assess, monitor and share other non-academic (but equally important) information, such as the acquisition and development of learning behaviours and the personal and social development of the children in our schools.

Trivium in the Sixth Form – the Colloquium Course

Martin Robinson's book *Trivium 21c* prompted an examination of the need to provide sixth-form students with a course that introduces them to the very basis of Western knowledge and experience. Discussions with Martin provoked profound issues which students should engage with, from the key philosophers to areas of human endeavour encompassing religion, philosophy, art, architecture, poetry, drama, fiction and science. To cover some of these areas in an effective way, the trivium structure would prove to be the most effective. Indeed, as Martin noted in his book, John of Salisbury (1120–1180) realized that the trivium showed the way to independent learning by the student initially understanding a subject and then being able to find solutions to the questions themselves (Robinson, 2013: 50).

Bay House's Colloquium course is developing from these initial ideas. Its core aim is true to its name, being an academic discussion that will enable learners to explore various notions, teachings or hypotheses by developing their own reasoned questioning and enquiry. The trivium structure is central to this aim. Students must be taught (grammar) the key points or aspects first, before going on to question and debate them (dialectic) with their peers. Having gained a solid grasp of the salient issues, students will then be able to develop their own responses to their chosen area of enquiry, and so communicate and present their reasoned position (rhetoric). This trivium structure of learning and knowing, followed by questioning and challenging, then finally on to the expression and synthesis, should ensure a robust introduction for our 16–18-year-olds to important aspects of Western knowledge.

The challenge for this new Colloquium course is to give students an overview of thought, discovery and experiment over the past 2,500 years in one period a week and in one term. It is vital that the students' own cultural capital is improved and increased, to enable them to be acquainted with the milestones of Western civilization. This lays the foundation for further enquiry and questioning. Colloquium will cover the key philosophers, theologians, commentators and scientists, to give students basic 'signposts' to point them towards further research. Embedded in the grammar and teaching will be the historical context of the notion or discovery, and so the student will gain an appreciation that belief, theory – and indeed knowledge – are all constructs. Central to this approach is for learners to know the methods behind knowledge and belief – that is, how and why people have arrived at their convictions or ideas. In addition, a key aim of the course is for students to sharpen their own methods of critical enquiry, reasoning and analysis so they can then employ these in any field of research. In this case Colloquium will be particularly suited to those students wishing to study EPQ, but also should be useful for any coursework component at A level.

The content of Colloquium is also informed by having over-arching questions that are used to give continuity and coherence. These include, what constitutes the best civilization? What has been lost or gained in a particular period? There is also scope to explore the cultural facets that make us human. The dialectic aspect of the course is assisted by a student-friendly question sheet which will help students to structure and formulate their reasoning and enquiry. Examples of these are: how do new ideas challenge previously held beliefs? How transformational were a set of new notions? How valid is a particular position in today's world? The initial grammar element begins with introductory sessions based upon the International Baccalaureate Theory of Knowledge course, to give students ideas and concepts around how knowledge is acquired. The main part of the taught element is broken down into a series of 'Minds' to introduce learners to the key periods of development of Western thought. These are the Ancient Mind (including Socrates, Plato and Aristotle), the Medieval Mind (including Christianity, Augustine, Luther), the Renaissance Mind (including Michelangelo and Galileo), the Enlightenment Mind (for example, Bentham) and the Scientific Mind (including Newton, Darwin and Einstein).

The structure of Colloquium mixes grammar and dialectic as, after each 'Mind' is taught, there is the opportunity for challenge and questioning. Students will have the chance to follow up the taught session with further reading and questioning that could include further extracts, research on

Google Scholar, to encourage an academic use of the internet, or a related episode on Radio 4's *In Our Time* series online. They would bring their further research and reflection to discuss in the next lesson. The role of the teacher (as a guide at this stage) is to ensure questioning is structured, relevant and develops a sense of reasoned scepticism to encourage deeper analysis and explanation. Again the model questions would help develop students' confidence and engagement in the discussions. The true Colloquium element of the course lies here, where students debate ideas and notions, with the teacher perhaps playing devil's advocate to challenge and extend thinking.

The final outcome of the Colloquium course is for students to discover their own area, or period, of interest, which will enable them to investigate an issue of their choosing for the final element of rhetoric (or expression). During the course, students should be developing the academic tools to tackle their chosen area of study (as they would for EPQ or a university dissertation), and be able to formulate and respond to their own question in the form of a presentation to their peers as well as a short piece of prose. Colloquium will give students an understanding of how ideas and constructs are formulated, and an appreciation of critical and reasoned approaches to discoveries and beliefs. It will also further their ability to weigh up an argument and develop their own perspective.

The Year 7 Developing Learning Programme

For a number of years, we have scheduled a period of time in our Year 7 curriculum for pupils to develop learning habits and skills. Through a range of different subject contexts and activities, our pupils acquire a greater understanding of what makes an effective learner, and their confidence has grown in their ability to practise these skills within their other subjects. The next phase in the evolution of this programme is to incorporate the principles of the trivium by introducing a challenge to the year group. Specifically, each pupil will deliver a speech, lasting roughly five minutes, in a public forum, on a subject of their choice. This project is being led by Andy Donn, one of our lead practitioners, working with two of our English teachers –

Jade Gordon and Glenn Tapp – in conjunction with Helen Jones, our Director of Performing Arts. The Developing Learning lessons provide the opportunities for pupils to learn about speech making and to analyse real-life examples (i.e. to acquire the knowledge (grammar) necessary to appreciate what is required of them). In addition, they will be taught the principles of argument and debate so that they can then apply these for themselves (dialectic). Through cross-curricular linking with their drama lessons, they will be able to learn how to deliver a speech effectively and to enhance their own skills of rhetoric. For pupils in our town, this experience is one that should enhance their knowledge, skill and confidence – and, in doing so, significantly enhance their cultural capital.

We are excited about the trivium developments that we are engaging with here at Bay House. Our journey, thus far, has demonstrated how our values are in synergy with the principles articulated in the trivium. Importantly, within our context, we strongly believe that focusing on these key principles, and closely aligning them with our school's aspirant culture, will ensure a curriculum that will challenge and encourage pupils and students to be more critical, creative and inquisitive. If this is supported by approaches to assessment that give learners a greater understanding of 'where they are at', then we can be more confident about their future success than we were under the less meaningful, more teacher-focused ascribing of 'levels'.

References

House of Commons (2012) Uncorrected Transcript Of Oral Evidence, Oral Evidence Taken Before The Education Committee, Reforming Key Stage 4 Qualifications (Wednesday 5 December). Available at: http://www.publications.parliament.uk/pa/cm201213/cmselect/cmeduc/uc808-i/uc80801.htm.

Robinson, Martin (2013) *Trivium 21c: Preparing Young People for the Future with Lessons from the Past.* Carmarthen: Independent Thinking Press.

Chapter 6

Slow Education, the Trivium and Eton College

Mike Grenier

In this chapter Mike makes connections between the key tenets of the Slow Education movement and the evolving nature of the trivium: at the heart of both is a respect for the student–teacher relationship and a strong belief in the need for a balanced, yet challenging, curriculum. An initial historical overview is followed by examples from schools that have promoted Slow Education, and connects their practice to the development of modern schooling at Eton College.

Mike is a House Master at Eton College, a Governor at Reed's School in Cobham and a Fellow of the Royal Society of Arts. In 2012 he co-founded the Slow Education movement in the United Kingdom. He has taught for over 20 years on Eton's Summer School programmes, and has also led sessions for the member schools of the Eton-Windsor-Slough State School Partnership. He also specializes in promoting greater coordination between academic and pastoral programmes, as well as leading staff development in the key areas of motivation, and creating and maintaining a school-wide ethos.

One of the lifelong lessons drummed into me during my education was the need to define terms in the introduction to an argument. Many litres of red ink have consequently been spilled down the margins of A4/comment boxes added by Microsoft Word during my 22 years as a teacher of English Literature and Language at Eton College. To avoid claims of hypocrisy or double standards – twin ghosts that stalk every teacher – I begin this chapter on 'Slow Education, the Trivium and Eton College' with a definition of the first part of what I consider to be a powerful triplet of phrases (or tricolon as the ancient rhetoricians would have it), confident that Martin Robinson has done more than enough over the past two years to redefine and update the second, and holding back my definition of the third for the sake of proportion.

What is Slow Education?

First, some amuse-bouches:

> We should always guide them (children) towards the best and most rewarding goals.
>
> Montaigne, 1533–1592

> Give a man knowledge and you give him the light to perceive and enjoy beauty, variety, surpassing ingenuity and majestic grandeur.
>
> W. Lovett and J. Collins, 1840

> The first cup is given by the master that teaches you to read and write and redeems you from ignorance, the second is given by the teacher of literature and equips you with learning, the third arms you with the eloquence of the rhetorician. Of these three cups most men drink. I, however, have drunk yet other cups at Athens – the imaginative draught of poetry, the clear draught of geometry, the

> sweet draught of music, the sharper draught of dialectic, and the nectar of all philosophy, whereof no man may ever drink enough.
>
> Apuleius, *c.*125–180 AD

It was after a particularly enjoyable dinner at an Italian restaurant aptly called L'Anima ('the soul') that the idea came to me of finding out if there was a parallel of the Slow Food movement in the world of education. I had seen a BBC documentary about the International Slow Food movement, which was started by Carlo Petrini, a food writer and political activist who was culturally offended to find the smell of McDonald's permeating the Spanish Steps in Rome. Slow Food combines a love of good produce, careful preparation of food, and the enjoyment that comes from the social act of sharing and consuming food. In many ways this echoes the trivium: knowing what to cook and how to cook it represents a fusion of grammar and logic, and the performance or rhetoric of presentation and consumption transforms nutrition into an art. I researched the concept online and found an article about Slow Education proposed by Maurice Holt, Emeritus Professor of Education at the University of Colorado in Denver (Holt, 2002). In an article that appeared in the American education journal *Phi Delta Kappan,* he made the connection between the production-line methods and poor end-product of fast food and much of what passed for modern schooling. This echoed my own experiences in the classroom. The arrival of another set of examinations (AS levels) in the lower sixth year at the turn of the millennium, combined with the modular nature of A level and GCSE examinations, had turned teaching in secondary schools into something that resembled an industrialized process. Teachers became obsessed with marking schemes and assessment objectives. Exam boards came around to schools with tempting INSET sessions to give you the 'inside track' on how to get the best out of your students, and students (as well as parents, senior leadership teams and government ministers) became dangerously fixated on performance over process.

In a review of his thinking in 2015, Maurice stated,

> The purpose of Slow Education is to improve the quality of teaching in our schools, by emphasizing the need for students to understand rather than merely memorize answers to predetermined questions.
>
> Our concern is with the process of education, with the ability of students to learn for themselves and from each other, rather than the regurgitation of right answers. We encourage team teaching, creative thinking and a climate of possibility and challenge, so as to advance the personal development of every student. To achieve this, students need time to reflect and argue, to explore and discover, to challenge and question. Hence the concept of Slow Education, and its relevance to the distinction between slow food and fast food.

While defining terms, I think it is important to review the word 'slow' in the context of education. It has been easy for those who disagree with our philosophy to say that the last thing we need is to take our foot off the pedal. We are already behind in the global race, our economy is struggling, and we need to accelerate in order to keep up with Shanghai and other 'superpowers' in the Organisation for Economic Cooperation and Development's Programme for International Student Assessment (PISA) tables. Slow Education, though, believes that the three pedals used to drive a car provide a perfect analogy for the way students and teachers can make long-lasting progress.

Each pedal has its own role and, although acceleration is sometimes the best way to make safe progress, at certain moments teachers and students need the brake to be pressed lightly, or for there to be a change of gear, in order to ensure difficult inclines are surmounted. Slowing down in order to learn safely – and, indeed, to see clearly what is ahead – strikes me as a crucial part of learning. One of the key thinkers whose ideas Maurice Holt introduced me to was the American statistician and management theorist

W. Edwards Deming (1900–1993). Maurice recognized an analogy between the obsession with measurement and outcomes in educational policy and Deming's view that too much business practice involved looking in the rear-view mirror; it is what is ahead and indeed some of the digressions to the side that offer a more stimulating vista and adventure. Thus 'slow' loses the pejorative sense that St Augustine (*c.*354–430) used when he recalled, 'If slow to learn, I was flogged.' It should be considered in relation to the distinction made by Roger Ascham (1515–1658) between 'hard wits', those who had intelligence and the ability to transfer their learning to new contexts, and 'quick wits', who were glib and superficial in their understanding.

In the words of Carl Honoré, whose book *In Praise of Slow* (2004) documents examples of slow practice from around the world and in other contexts than simply education: 'Fast and Slow do more than just describe a rate of change. They are shorthand for ways of being or philosophies of life' (Honoré, 2004: 14).

What, then, is the relationship between Slow Education and the trivium? Here a distinction needs to be drawn between what is taught and how it is taught, between curriculum and pedagogy. What is also very much at the heart of the evolution of the trivium is the question: what is education for? If dialectic is not to descend into the sort of quibbling and pedantry that Aristophanes (*c.*446–386BCE) mocks in *The Clouds,* it needs to have either a philosophical purpose and seek to define what is good or true, or a social purpose for the improvement of the state of mankind, or both. Slow Education seeks this dual purpose. If the purpose of rhetoric is to learn how to use language well, then, like the Lyceum of Isocrates (436–338BCE), Slow Education will emphasize the significance of not only facility of expression but also relevance, and students and teachers will continuously appraise their own performance as well as that of others. Deliberate practice and carefully judged feedback are crucial to ensure that rhetoric (in whatever form it takes) avoids being the 'empty babble' that Montaigne experienced. And the pursuit of knowledge needs to be with the aim of seeking out fuller understanding. In Slow Education, grammar and knowledge are active parts of the process; parts of a complex organic relationship that allow deep thinking and creativity to flourish. Superficial knowledge is no better than empty rhetoric or false logic, and in creating a stimulating and engaging curriculum it is equally important that time is made flexible, which requires thoughtful timetabling as well as sensitive classroom management, so that the constant interaction between the three parts of the trivium can work. Time is, therefore, the catalyst. Thus Trivium 21c and Slow Education seek a synthesis of the past and the present, of knowledge and skills, and of quality of instruction and of learning.

The Slow Teacher

When medieval society was looking for a type of schooling that would see Church and State flourish again in the liberal arts, it cherry-picked what it felt was appropriate from the classical world. The trivium was what was needed by a select few; Slow Education, on the other hand, is comprehensive and seeks to allow all students to engage with their learning in a meaningful and lifelong manner. A modern democracy that is engaged in a plural conversation about its own character, values and identity requires something more open than the medieval authorities would have allowed. The Slow teacher must be free from dogma but wary of the lazy free-for-all that represents an abuse of the term 'liberal'. The Slow teacher must also be allowed to ensure that the tradition (in the classical world) of the primacy of relations between teacher and pupil is maintained. The upbringing of both Achilles and Alexander the Great was entrusted to a tutor, and the intense relationship fostered respectively by Chiron and Aristotle (384–322BCE) was based on another triad: in this case, the development of moral virtues, the ethical mentoring of a young student by a wise teacher, and an education, the purpose of which was to be both useful and relevant. The nature of the teacher is not often alluded to in the theories of the past, but there are a number of voices who seek to define this while also exploring the philosophical debates about the purpose of education. Developing good character and conduct are at the heart of an effective education, and this education is the ambition of schools, families and communities – it is not simply up to teachers to impart virtue and assume that it will be soaked up by willing students. The ambition of Slow teachers is to follow the advice of Quintilian (35–*c.*96):

> The excellence of the teacher is to identify differences in talents of pupils.
>
> '*Virtuo preceptoris est ingeniorum notare discrimina*'
> – quoted in Little, 2015: 36

These words were uncovered in one of the ancient classrooms at Eton College during a recent restoration, and they leave me optimistic that 16th-century teachers had an interest in a compassionate and humane education. The Slow teacher must be allowed to become a virtuoso, skilfully knowing which tempo to apply to ensure that students are neither lagging behind nor driven to apathy by inaction. Daniel Willingham, a Professor of Cognitive Psychology at the University of Virginia, boils down years of reading student surveys of academic staff into two key qualities – the teacher who is well prepared and who cares is the one who is most highly rated by her students (Willingham, 2009). This onus on the teacher was made easier in the classical world by the private nature of tuition. A one-to-one relationship allows the virtuoso a better chance to gauge progress. Class sizes do matter if your ambition is to develop strong relationships and allow effective mentoring to occur. Students in smaller classes also have more opportunity to have their voices heard and their ideas debated.

In its evolution, the three-legged stool that is the trivium has lost a couple of legs regularly – for example, when rhetoric was viewed with suspicion and seen as fomenting dissidence, and when grammar was seen as promoting pagan classical texts over the objective truths of logic. The most effective and balanced relationship between teacher and student will occur when all three legs create stability and balance. The virtuoso not only knows the content of his subject, but also knows the methods that are best suited to communicating with his students; he needs to develop systems and structures that are both rigorous and efficient; and he should know how much impact he can have through verbal and non-verbal communication, either orally, in reporting or in feedback that students can follow in order to progress. I would argue strongly that there are many triviums for schools to consider – the intersection of three routes and the public meeting place of the schoolroom is relevant to teachers as much as it is to students, to pedagogy as much as it is to the curriculum. A Slow trivium school will allow its teachers to develop, to practise and to share in effective and engaging methods. It is this sort of model that has recently been developed in the Blackburn Slow Education network. Here a group of primary schools has reflected on their own practice and, with the help of Dr Phil Wood from the University of Leicester and Joe Harrison-Greaves, a co-founder of the Slow Education movement and an educational consultant in the north-west of England, has embarked on research projects that aim to give teachers new grammar, new logic and a new rhetoric.

Developing this sort of research allows schools and teachers to engage in a dialectic. If teachers expect their students to follow the advice of Abelard (1079–1142), they need to practise what they preach:

> Constant questioning is the first key to wisdom. For through doubt we are led to inquiry, and by inquiry we discern the truth.

Collaboration and sharing best practice are now seen as important to ensuring continuing professional development in teachers. Juan Luis Vives (1493–1540) required teachers to meet four times a year to discuss the mental qualities of their students so that they could determine the curriculum best suited to their individual dispositions. The Jesuit tradition under Aquaviva (1543–1615) required teachers to be taught by experts in their fields once they had proved themselves to be sufficiently knowledgeable about their subject. This form of training covered methods in 'reading, teaching, writing, correcting and managing a class'.

Keeping teachers abreast of new research and new methods has become a lucrative business in recent years with schools devoting a great deal of time and money to continuing professional development (CPD). Some has gone into the pockets of what might loosely be called quack consultants, but recently greater use of educational research to inform good teaching has seen a marked improvement in the effectiveness of CPD to allow teachers to improve their skills and competence.

Much of a teacher's success will result from skilful communication, and it is in this area that rhetoric is key. One of the key topics taught in A level English Language is conversation theory, and one of the main theorists is H. P. Grice (1913–1988). After studying hours of recorded social interaction, he came to the conclusion that four maxims were crucial to successful communication (or what he termed cooperative principles) (Grice, 1975):

Manner	maintaining the most helpful order and structure in what we say
Quality	truthfulness or accuracy
Quantity	when to lecture, to talk, to prompt, or in fact to say nothing
Relevance	sticking to the topic

These four maxims strike me as being essential for a Slow teacher. You can observe many hours of lessons and see these maxims being followed or ignored. The Slow teacher knows when to adapt her manner according to the concepts of classical rhetoric: skilful exposition, rhetorical questioning, proposing a false concept, appealing to ethos or pathos. In terms of quantity, it is fascinating to see how many teachers learn over the years when brevity is the soul of wit – a quick retort can defuse a potential behavioural crisis, and a snappy report can easily embed itself in the mind of a vulnerable student. One of the projects in the Blackburn Research Network, conducted at St Silas CE Primary School, allowed children to investigate a series of problems for themselves, with teachers observing the students as they worked out the problem. This is the active use of silence by a teacher, and one of the key skills of the virtuoso – it is often best to allow things to develop and evolve organically, at their own pace, rather than to interrupt. I would also recommend silence in the classroom to allow introverts to think and write, and for hard wits to shine against quick wits. This is what I would define as the rhetoric of the Slow teacher, and it comes as a result of a teacher's confidence in the steady accumulation of knowledge, experience, and the chance to use reason and logic to determine effective practice.

Slow Students and the Trivium

Returning to Professor Holt's definition above, the Slow trivium expects its students 'to reflect and argue, to explore and discover, to challenge and question'. This is another powerful triad of cognitive tasks, and it takes time to develop them in each student. But time is on the side of all teachers if the process becomes more important than the content: the long-term benefits of teaching skills and habits of mind outweigh the short-termism of fact-based regurgitation. I would like all my students to learn skills that they can adapt to different contexts both in and out of the classroom, and throughout their adult lives. I would also like them to be able to see that learning is a social phenomenon and not to feel that it is about the individual against the system. Again, this is an area where Deming's PDSA model (Plan-Do-Study-Act) and his '14 Points for the Transformation of Management' (see Deming, 1986) provide important advice about successful models in business – the useful and productive worker must feel that he can contribute to the success of the system, and the system must be prepared to reward quality of work and craftsmanship above all else. For many students in England, their engagement with their studies resembles the dehumanizing experience of the factory worker in Charlie Chaplin's *Modern Times*. Compliance with externally determined criteria leads to demotivation and a diminution of imagination and intellectual ambition. Teenagers are especially vulnerable to the limitations posed by extrinsic motivation, and there is nothing more soul-destroying for me, as a teacher, than having to explain to a bright, excited intellect that he needs to rein it in and do what the examiner wants and the marking scheme demands.

I have been fortunate enough to meet John Abbott, whose book *Overschooled But Undereducated* has had a profound impact on my thinking. John's view is that the English and American systems have gone 'against the grain of the brain' in ignoring the intrinsic curiosity of human beings (Abbott, 2010: 211). He finds many powerful voices to support his view that keeping children at an arm's length from actually experiencing their education is counter-productive:

> Tell me, and I forget;
>
> Show me, and I remember;
>
> Let me do, and I understand.
>
> Confucius

> Time was also (as an infant) I knew no Latin; but this I learned without fear or suffering, by mere observation, amid the caresses of my nursery and jests of friends, smiling and sportively encouraging me. This I learned without any pressure of punishment to urge me on, for my heart urged me to give birth to its conceptions which I could only do by learning words not of those who taught, but of those who talked with me; in whose ears also I gave birth to the thoughts, whatever I conceived. No doubt, then, that a free curiosity has more force in our learning these things, than a frightful enforcement.
>
> St Augustine, 354–430

> If a school sends out children with the desire for knowledge and some idea of how to acquire and use it, it will have done its work. Too many leave school with the appetite killed and the mind loaded with undigested lumps of information.
>
> Sir Richard Livingstone, 2013 [1941]: 29

Doing, acting on the senses, using scientific methods, acting, writing, composing – these are the practical expressions of human intellect that the Slow trivium embraces. It would, though, be incorrect to assume that there is no place for the grammar associated with these forms. Let me take the act of creative writing and suggest that it is the interaction between the three strands of the trivium that is crucial. First, children must learn to love language, to admire its tricksy spirit, and to play with it. The more confident they become when handling this difficult stuff, the better. It is akin to play-dough or making fresh pasta – initially fiddly and in danger of becoming a shapeless blob but, with experience and dexterity, capable of being moulded into all sorts of shapes. Literacy projects and the desire to improve standards have driven the fun out of language. The Slow student needs to play with verse forms, to speak aloud, to listen to audio books, to play Scrabble, to play the Uxbridge English Dictionary game from *I'm Sorry I Haven't a Clue*, to write a story without the letter 'l', and any other such nonsense. Formal grammar needs to be brought to life using far more scientific methods of observation – spot the verb; work out what that word is doing, then label it; comment on the language choice of great writers, and copy them. 'We murder to dissect' was Wordsworth's damning phrase – there is too much learning associated with language and grammar that is autopsy rather than sensationalist observation or Archimedes-like experiment. Language should feed the senses, then the heart, and then enter into the 'purer mind'. If this seems frivolous, Francis Bacon (1561–1626), that key proponent of the scientific method, wrote to Sir Henry Savile (1549–1622), Provost of Eton, advising him of five key points in his 'Discourse Touching Helps for the Intellectual Powers': 'That exercises are to be framed to the life; that is to say to work ability in that kind whereof a man in the course of action shall have the most use.'

Bacon also saw the benefit of the slow and steady accumulation of skills by practice, as this would lead to swifter application when mastery was achieved. He describes this as initially learning 'to do things well and clean; after, promptly and readily'. The Slow student needs to be taken carefully and deliberately through stages of learning with an end in sight: independence, self-motivation, as a result of custom and habit producing perfection. Neuroscience has made it clear in recent years that the steady accumulation of new information and skills is cemented by regular reviewing. The fast processes of many lessons leave little time for the sort of deliberate reflection that is required to allow knowledge to turn into understanding.

Bacon's 'helps' are enacted in schools across the country, some of whom have become connected with the Slow Education network. Both St Silas in Blackburn and Carterhatch Infant School in Enfield, north London, have reviewed the way their young children learn, and have looked to reverse-engineer their provision so that students who leave their schools are capable from a young age of developing their own interests, researching independently in order to make their work 'well and clean', and also becoming aware of when they need help from their teachers in order to make progress. In a film, made by Fully Formed Films and featured on the Slow Education website (http://sloweducation.co.uk/videos/), these principles are defined in action at Carterhatch Infant School by Anna Ephgrave, Assistant Head of Early Years Foundation Stage:

> If children are engaged, they are learning; instead of rushing the children through their stages to meet their targets, we actually believe children develop at their own pace and in their own unique way ... The work the children are doing is very ambitious and quite sophisticated; we've provided an environment in which every child can pursue his own interests.

The echoes with Quintilian's philosophy are unmistakable, and what is more the school itself is rated as Outstanding by Ofsted. The balance here is between students who become powerfully self-motivated and teachers who have high expectations as well as sensitivity. At St Silas the focus is on 'challenges', with the children allowed regulated freedom to work in areas of the classroom designated 'Research', 'Creative', 'Language' and 'STEM – Science, Technology, Engineering, Maths'. Reviewing their practice, the teachers have sought to create opportunities for deeper learning, to move away from 'cut and paste' research and the superficial acquisition of information.

There is a strong historical tradition of this sort of Slow study in which the personal engagement of the students and the intensity of their experiences leads to deeper knowledge and understanding. Pestalozzi (1746–1827) proposed the significance of '*Anschauung*' (personal experience from sense impressions), and his theories were taken up by the philosopher and teacher Herbart (1776–1841), whose use of a demonstration school so neatly echoes the way that St Silas has opened its doors to teachers across the country who are keen to see its enhanced continuous provision in action. The recently opened Centre for Innovation and Research in Learning at Eton College, in effect a research laboratory embedded within the school, is also a space that is open to teachers from the UK and around the world. Herbart promoted the importance of absorption (or deeper learning) and reflection in learning, and it is the aim of the Slow student to experience both. This needs to be given time in the working week, of course. Timetabling is crucial in terms of creating the right sort of culture for deeper learning, and the 'tyranny of the school bell' is the enemy of the Slow student.

The Slow School

Slow teachers and Slow students combine to create a dynamic environment I will define as the Slow school. Slow schools are places where learning is paramount, and they are also environments in which trial and error are not only allowed, but actively encouraged. They open their doors to new ideas, reflect on their recent innovations, seek to refine and improve – above all, they are never complacent.

When taking the long view, the history of the trivium in England is of similarly constant evolution and innovation, although acceleration has been much more rapid in the past century. The new knowledge released by Renaissance Humanism and the scientific adventures of the Enlightenment saw schools and universities slowly re-create and reorganize themselves in order to prepare their students to belong to new and changing social structures. Heated debates over the curriculum saw schools move from the classical model to a more modern one in the late 19th and early 20th century, and in recent years the debate over the balance between grammar, logic and rhetoric has resurfaced, with new information from neuroscience as well as the innovations that ICT has brought to both teachers and students.

A school that embraces Slow Education will be like Vittorino da Feltre's (1378–1446) La Casa Giocosa or 'House of Joy'. Joy in learning and joy in participating must be at the heart of the human and emotional drama of schooling. Joyous engagement echoes one of Deming's principles, Joy in work. There should be nothing controversial about this, but if you ask many students how they feel about their learning, especially at secondary school, 'joy' is likely to be near the bottom of the list. It does not have to be this way, of course, and it is especially sad that so many adolescents find themselves under so much pressure to perform that their mental and physical health is impaired. To me, adolescence is the most exciting of times – a period when knowledge and experience begin to create a powerful double helix. In his 1904 work *Adolescence,* Granville S. Hall (1844–1924) sounds a warning Jeremiah would have been proud of:

> Youth is awakening to a new world, and understands neither it, nor itself [...] Increasingly urban life with its temptations, sedentary occupations and passive stimuli, had come to dominate just when an active life was most needed. (Quoted in Abbott, 2010: 129)

What he would have made of 4G phones and Wi-Fi access can be left to the imagination. However, for thousands of years the point has been made that young people need stimulation and they need the chance to be actively involved in their learning. To argue against this idea is to stand dogmatically against the wisdom of most civilizations as well as a good deal of physiological and neuroscientific knowledge.

Another example of a place of learning that has sought to break free from the industrialized model is Matthew Moss High School in Rochdale. It is a school that is wrestling with the best way to engage its students while also ensuring that they make effective progress in terms of their understanding of subject knowledge. One way that it has responded to the former issue is to develop its 'My World' project-based learning programme, described in an OECD report as follows (OECD, 2013):

> The 'My World' curriculum at Matthew Moss High School targets students in grade 7 and 8, who spend one day per week throughout the school year on project work. Teachers introduce the projects to the students, and then students work self-directly [*sic*] forming teams, gathering possibilities and writing a project plan for approval, before conducting the project. The teachers act as facilitators, presenting in-time lessons or suggesting additional sources of knowledge (e.g., lessons in other departments). There is regular ongoing feedback, and a final exhibition of results to teachers and parents is part of the assessment. Students receive individual written evaluation reports.

The Slow methodology here allows for all features of the trivium to be embedded in the working week of learners (the school avoids speaking about 'students' or 'pupils') new to the school. It is informed by some of the methodologies of postgraduate research, and there are a couple of features of the curriculum that have always struck me as allowing the combination of absorption and reflection. The first is encouraging an interdisciplinary approach. For example, a learner who is producing a project on the history of her house is able to explore the building methods of the 19th century, to consider the nature of housing before and during the Industrial Revolution, to place a living space in the context of social and economic history while also learning how to use public documents and Land Registry details in order to make a verifiable timeline. Cutting and pasting from Google this is not. When it comes to presentation, learners are able to review and redraft in order to refine and improve their work, again a crucial skill of any craftsman and something now removed from formal assessment in many GCSEs and A levels. They must also perform well in a viva, and this sort of live presentation ensures that oral skills are connected to knowledge, and that the ability to think on your feet is a key quality. If those assessing come from outside the school community, such as professional architects or lecturers at local universities, then the connection between the learner and the worlds of work or higher education are strengthened. Slow schools do not exist in a cloistered or gated bubble.

Style and quality matter, and in the past they informed many of the exercises in the trivium. The addition of the Quadrivium (arithmetic, geometry, music and astronomy) not only expanded the range of disciplines that formed part of what should be known, but there began to be greater focus on performance and the quality of work. The Slow school embraces the concept of what Adam Smith (1723–1790) described as the 'alert intelligence of the craftsmen' (quoted in Abbott, 2010: 91). In preparing students for the complexities and rapidly shifting socioeconomic realities of the 21st century we must value flexibility of thinking, quality of preparation and depth of engagement more than ever. With many of the simpler 'white collar' tasks being outsourced either to developing countries or becoming automated by increasingly sophisticated computer processes, it strikes me that a Slow approach to learning is the best way to give the human mind the dispositions and habits required to thrive and flourish.

The other key area in which Slow schools are important is in offering a healthier experience for children in an age when mental health among English schoolchildren is in an increasingly fragile state. I often refer to the difference between battery-farmed students and free-range learners when speaking about pastoral care in schools. Within a few minutes of visiting a school, you can pick up the mood and the enthusiasm of the place. Recently I visited Gallions Primary School at the very end of the Docklands Light Railway in the East of London in Beckton. The school is built on a disused gas storage facility and is at the perimeter of a very disadvantaged housing estate. Inside, rather like the Tardis, a hub of activity reveals itself to you as you walk its corridors. All pupils play musical instruments; artwork is on display everywhere; reading in a well-stocked library during the morning is part of the culture; outside there is the most tranquil garden, planted with scented herbs and shrubs to create a quiet place for reflection; and there are zones for physical activity and growing vegetables, along with plenty of mud and sand. Many of the pupils are the most proficient English speakers in their families; many of them come from extremely disadvantaged backgrounds, and it is at school that they have the harmony and the peace in order to thrive. Anxiety levels are down; the emotional barometer of the place ensures that the parts of the brain that need calm in order for learning to take place and ideas to embed themselves are able to act efficiently. This is not to say that it is quiet all the time, but the Slow school knows the difference between creative noise and meaningless hubbub.

Later that week I went up the M11 to St John's College Preparatory School in Cambridge, a private school whose pupils generally come from social and economic backgrounds of far greater privilege than those in Gallions. However, the drama playing out in front of me was almost identical. Happy, confident and purposeful students were actively engaging in their tasks in the classroom. Small groups – and this is why class sizes do matter in the Slow movement – were able to enter into prolonged dialogue with their teachers and with their peers. There was clearly a philosophical culture of enquiry, induction and deduction at work, and the teachers knew when to follow Augustine's advice to talk with pupils. There was much active listening, but also a good deal of subtle prompting and timely correcting. And when the bell came for break-time the children dashed out, ran around, played the games they had either invented or inherited from earlier generations, and some came running up to the head teacher, Kevin Jones, and told him stories and jokes, or held his hand.

The healthy culture created by the teachers at both these schools allows young people to flourish. The classical tradition of allowing these pupils the chance to learn, to feel, to reason and to participate actively in their education has been updated for the modern age. I have often been asked, though, whether the primary school years are when Slow methods work best. Thomas Gray's (1716–1771) melancholic 'Ode on a Distant Prospect of Eton College' springs to mind, as he looked down from the peaks of mid-life pessimism and saw future generations of Etonians on the fields:

> Alas, regardless of their doom,
>
> The little victims play!

There has been a good deal of research over the years in the world of social psychology about the twin impact of (a) the transition from primary to secondary school and (b) adolescence. This is a dangerous time, full of stress and strain, and the Slow trivium can provide stability as well as continuity.

Slow schools genuinely place the well-being of their students at the core of their academic and co-curricular provision. The work was started by Ian Morris at Wellington College in Berkshire, England, and spread across the country by teachers who visit his workshops. It provides an example of a measured and thoughtful approach to what follows in the footsteps of the Greek philosophical pursuit of 'eudaimonia'. Giving teachers and pupils alike the opportunity to learn how to recognize moments of deep engagement and to seek out meaning in their actions is critical in the pursuit of the good life.

The work of Seligman, Lyubomirsky, Sheldon and Schkade in the field of positive psychology, summarized the factors that determine a person's happiness in the following formula:

> H (Happiness) = S (biological set point) + C (context or circumstances) + V (voluntary acts or intentional activity)

There is little schools can do about the 'S' part of the equation, but they can provide environments, experiences and opportunities that create the right biosphere for healthy personal development. One of the limitations of the medieval trivium was its lack of flexibility and its narrow focus; the modern, Slow trivium allows much more freedom for personal engagement, so that voluntary action and self-motivation become the norm for students. What the philosopher Michael Oakeshott (1901–1990) described as the slow and painful progress of thinking that can make the human condition burdensome is made much more manageable, both intellectually and psychologically, when the dialogue remains open, fluid and eager to embrace change. Thus the Slow school avoids dogma and seeks educational experiences that cannot be mechanistically judged by narrow assessment objectives.

The Slow school is liberal and liberating, using knowledge and deeper understanding to engage in debate, reflection, argument and a pursuit of the good life. It offers the chance to 'respond to the invitation of the great intellectual adventures in which human beings have come to display their various understandings—of the world and of themselves' (Oakeshott, 1989: 32).

This type of plural, healthily sceptical and open-minded environment is just what a Slow school is about, and it is founded on the principles of thinkers and practitioners from across the centuries. Its roots are in a powerful synthesis of the trivium, a modern understanding of how children learn, and a recognition of the limitations of an industrialized model of schooling that has stifled creativity, enjoyment and ambition for too long.

What About Eton College?

Martin Robinson finished *Trivium 21c* with the following quotation from William Cory (1823–1892), a much revered poet and Eton Master. It can be found on the Eton College website:

> At school you are engaged not so much in acquiring knowledge as in making mental efforts under criticism … you go to a great school not so much for knowledge as for arts and habits; for the habit of attention, for the art of expression, for the art of assuming at a moment's notice a new intellectual position, for the art of entering quickly into another person's thoughts, for the habit of submitting to censure and refutation, for the art of indicating assent or dissent in graduated terms, for the habit of regarding minute points of accuracy, for the art of working out what is possible in a given time, for taste, for discrimination, for mental courage, and for mental soberness.

These habits and arts belong very much to the Slow tradition, and will inform any school that has the development of the whole person as its core purpose. All the schools that I have visited in the past four years during my adventure throughout England have sought to foster these virtues in all their students. At Eton and similar private schools, much is made of tradition – the past informs the present, we've been doing *x* and *y* for centuries – but it is often a sense of tradition that is conservative rather than progressive. When the trivium was reinvented in the Middle Ages at Eton it is striking to see how class sizes and teacher:pupil ratios changed. At first the school contained 25 scholars and one Master. Henry VI, the school's founder, made it clear that – unlike a monastic institution – his school would need a classroom. The Cloisters, though, were used for public disputation by the scholars. When Eton followed the model of Winchester College and increased its student body to 70, an Usher was appointed to support the Master for the purposes of teaching. Older students then acted as monitors, similar in many ways to classroom assistants. Much of the learning involved translating and working on language exercises, and a passive approach to grammar was very much king. As a counterbalance, once a year the scholars were, like Feste in *Twelfth Night,* allowed to play the fool, and bawdy and scurrilous lyrics were penned. The monotony of the regular holy days was broken when the boys chose from among their body the 'Episcopus Nihilensis' (Bishop of Nothingness) and when in September, in a lovely echo of Wordsworth, they would go nutting and return with their spoils in a riot of colourful clothing. By and large, though, there was little variety in the curriculum, and it was left to the scholars to write creatively and debate in their spare time. This is a key part of the culture of the school, and any attempt to infuse a school with the trivium needs to take into account what should be part of a centrally determined curriculum and what should be student-led. As Eton grew in the 17th century a larger schoolroom, Upper School, was built and to this day stands as a monument to a method of pedagogy that is still in operation in parts of the world where the student is expected to sit and quietly engage with exercises and rote learning. The ratio of teacher to students was an eye-watering 1:50 – certainly cheap, but it required a combination of strict corporal punishment and an acceptance of the occasional riot for the school to operate. Eton remained very much in this mould until the middle of the 19th century, and it would be fair to summarize its relationship with the tenets of *Trivium 21c* and Slow Education as negligible.

What strikes me as important about Eton since then is that it has remained actively engaged in an argument about its values, its curriculum and its purpose. In the middle of the 19th century, in order to bring the school into line with the early Victorian age, Prince Albert funded prizes in modern European languages, and a privately funded mathematical school was established in order to prepare Etonians either for their studies at university or for a career in the army. The Clarendon Report (a Royal Commission that looked into the governance as well as the academic and pastoral standards of schools such as Eton (quoted in Shrosbree, 1988, pp. 32–33)) states:

> Before the year 1836 there appears to have been no mathematical teaching of any kind at Eton.

Eton Masters were similar to tutors, and the idea of a specialist teacher of mathematics as opposed to a general teacher of writing and arithmetic was simply anathema. However, Stephen Hawtrey pioneered the mathematical school as an extra which parents would sign up for. By 1851 it had become part of the mainstream school. Hawtrey's vision of pedagogical practice has interesting echoes with modern practices. He had an early belief in what is now called 'flipping' lessons – work was done away from the classroom prior to the lesson, and the Master would then use lesson time to check the pupil's understanding and progress, and individualize the provision. He was keen to report periodically on his pupils, with his aim being to track both their industry and progress. With class sizes of 10 or 12, he was able to treat each student according to his ability. Quintilian would have approved.

It seems that the modern subjects such as languages, geography and natural sciences had a powerful impact on the nature of teaching at Eton. Whereas the grammar lessons of the formal trivium involved large numbers of boys copying out, rote learning or translating chunks of classical texts into English, the new subjects required a more practical, hands-on approach. The number of Masters Eton employed grew and in the early 20th century another battle was fought that predates C. P. Snow's thesis contained in 'The Two Cultures'. The Head Master at the time, E. C. Lyttelton, was concerned that the compulsory studying of Greek was limiting Etonians' exposure to modern subjects. He noted, in correspondence that is now housed in the Eton College library, that Etonians were particularly alert to current affairs and political studies, but that there was little chance to study these fully. He was also deeply concerned that during the course of their five years at the school, many Etonians made no progress in Greek, whereas they may have been excellent in subjects not part of the formal curriculum. He believed that:

> ... if a learner is growing intellectually it is because he is solving problems, not simply being confronted with them, nor being told the answer.

He wanted more Etonians to be fully engaged with their learning, and he was a champion of the proper study of English literature, seeing it as 'the best hope of stirring in them some idea of literary beauty'. I owe him my job.

His views met with some pretty forthright objections, and for a variety of reasons. One critic claimed that 'a modern side might temporarily make the School more popular, but would eventually lower its prestige. It would certainly appeal to a different class of parent.' Another Master wrote to the Provost, effectively the Chairman of Governors:

> The plan to move to the Modern will see a transference of power from the abler to the inferior man on the staff ... I asked the Head Master this morning if he could imagine any modern man on the staff writing a book or poem really worth reading. They have not got any literary inspiration: the majority of the classical staff has.

Why is this debate from 1910 of any relevance to Eton, Slow Education and the trivium? I would argue that it gets to the heart of what matters in a school: what students learn and how, and the educational philosophy that underpins both curriculum and pedagogy. At no stage was Lyttelton seeking to 'lower standards' – in fact, he was driven by the powerful force that makes strong head teachers, namely the ambition to allow all the students in his care to make the very most of their talents. He expresses this beautifully in a memorandum to his governing body that shows me just how deeply his thinking is connected with the ideas of the past, the very ideas that inform Slow Education and *Trivium 21c*:

> Another reason [for adopting the modern curriculum], and educationally the strongest of all is the necessity of providing, for the slower and the quicker alike, more individual teaching, not for the

> purpose of giving more but less help; of securing that the boys grapple with difficulties in a hopeful spirit, being encouraged and guided to the right extent.

Eton in the 21st century has opened its doors to students from different cultures and backgrounds in order to offer them its education and to gain from them the new points of view and intellectual positions that William Cory saw as being at the heart of a good school. Similarly, the past 50 years have seen a good deal of change in the nature of the teaching staff, with much the same effect. Etonians were once exclusively taught by Old Etonians, and the dangers of conservatism, narrow-mindedness and a limited exposure to new thinking were very real. In those days it was not so much an adventure; more like a strictly timetabled guided tour, with little chance for exploration. Eton now finds itself part of a national system of education that Lyttelton would not have recognized. Its teachers and students have to work their way through what is effectively a mass-produced examination in two out of the five years that the students spend at the school. It is, however, in the manner of teaching and the life outside the classroom that a truer flavour of the modern trivium exists. Students are encouraged to enter academic prizes that largely ignore the narrowness of the national curriculum. Many volunteer to run societies, inviting speakers from all around the country to come and speak on their areas of personal expertise for an hour in the evening. Others have willingly offered to help in community service projects with local charities and in mentoring programmes with local state schools. The full co-curricular provision also allows for a good deal of performance – music, drama and sport ensure that most Etonians experience the fuller education that the Athenian state saw as being crucial to the health of the body politic.

Perhaps the least known but most important part of Eton life that connects the school to the trivium and Slow Education is what is called 'Private Business'. Each student is part of a tutorial group of six students, and he has a tutor for his first three years until he joins the sixth form, at which point he writes a letter of application to a member of the teaching staff with whom he feels he can develop a positive, lasting academic and pastoral relationship. This takes us back to the strong relationships between Aristotle and Alexander the Great: an intense bond between tutor and pupil which has little fixed curriculum but the unstated purpose of developing intellectual skills, opening the mind to new ideas with no threat of examination, and seeking to discuss some of the key concerns of living the good life in the great philosophical traditions of ancient Greece. In the past year I have run a 'Private Business' group that has contained four Etonians and three students from St Joseph's Catholic High School in Slough. The intellectual freedom that all have enjoyed, and the positive way that they have responded over the year, has made it clear to me that open questioning, free-range learning and an educational structure based on process, rather than content, provides just the sort of stimulation that young people need in the 21st century. In returning to the essential precepts of the trivium, these students, their teacher and I have found ourselves revived and reinvigorated. In this small group we have met the intellectual challenges that Lyttelton sought for all his Etonians, and enjoyed what John Milton (1608–1674) called 'a complete and generous education'.

References

Abbott, John with MacTaggart, Heather (2010) *Overschooled But Undereducated: How the Crisis in Education is Jeopardizing our Adolescents*. London: Continuum.

Deming, W. Edwards (1986) *Out of the Crisis*. Cambridge, MA: Massachusetts Institute of Technology, Center for Advanced Engineering Study.

Grice, H. Paul (1975) 'Logic and conversation'. In Peter Cole and Jerry L. Morgan (eds), *Studies in Syntax and Semantics III: Speech Acts*. New York: Academic Press, pp. 183–198.

Holt, Maurice (2002) 'It's Time to Start the Slow School Movement,' *Phi Delta Kappan*, 84: 264–271.

Honoré, Carl (2004) *In Praise of Slow*. London: Orion Books.

Little, Tony (2015) *An Intelligent Person's Guide to Education*. London: Bloomsbury.

Livingstone, Richard (2013 [1941]) *On Education*. Cambridge: Cambridge University Press.

Lyubomirsky, Sonja, Sheldon, Kennon M., Schkade, David (2005) 'Pursuing happiness: The architecture of sustainable change', *Review of General Psychology*, Vol 9(2), Jun 2005, 111–131. Available at: http://dx.doi.org/10.1037/1089-2680.9.2.111.

Oakeshott, Michael (1989) 'A Place of Learning.' In Timothy Fuller (ed.), *The Voice of Liberal Learning: Michael Oakeshott on Education*. New Haven, CT: Yale University Press, pp. 17–42.

OECD (2013) *Innovative Learning Environment Project: Universe Case*. Available at: http://www.oecd.org/edu/ceri/49773187.pdf.

O'Hear, Anthony and Sidwell, Marc (2009) *The School of Freedom*. Exeter: Imprint Academic.

Seligman, Martin (2002) *Authentic Happiness*. New York, NY: The Free Press.

Shrosbree, Colin (1988) *Public Schools and Private Education: The Clarendon Commission, 1861–64, and the Public Schools Acts*. Manchester: Manchester University Press.

Willingham, Daniel (2009) *Why Don't Students Like School? A Cognitive Scientist Answers Questions about How the Mind Works and What it Means for the Classroom*. San Francisco, CA: Jossey-Bass.

Chapter 7

The Trivium and Human Cultural Evolution

Nick Rose

Nick spent over 12 years as a teacher working in state schools, initially teaching science then gradually drifting towards teaching A level and GCSE psychology, before finally becoming a leading practitioner for psychology and research. In 2013 he started a blog, 'Evidence into Practice', which explores how psychological and educational research might be applied to the classroom. He was shortlisted for the TES Schools award for 'Teacher Blogger of the Year' in 2015. He now works for Teach First as part of the Knowledge Development team.

Nick is fascinated by the idea that we might be able to apply some of the principles of evolution through natural selection to the realm of culturally transmitted ideas. In this chapter, he gives a brief 'natural history' of education and examines how grammar, dialectic and rhetoric might be understood in light of the processes of inheritance, selection and variation which operate at the heart of evolutionary systems. He admits many of these ideas are speculative, but presents them as a thought-provoking metaphor for fans of the trivium.

> And then he said to me – this is honestly true – he said to me, 'Well, you can prove anything with facts, can't you?'
>
> For a minute, I went, 'Yeah.' And then I thought, 'Hang on! That's the most fantastic way of winning an argument I've ever heard! "You can ... I'm not interested in facts. I find they tend to cloud my judgement. I prefer to rely on instinct and blind prejudice."'
>
> Stewart Lee, *How I Escaped my Certain Fate*: 82

Before I joined teaching, I worked with the psychologist and writer Susan Blackmore as a postgraduate research assistant. My 'day job' involved parapsychology, but my own research interests quickly became dominated by the concept of cultural evolution, especially the idea of memes ('cultural replicators' first described by Richard Dawkins in *The Selfish Gene* (1976), and explored brilliantly by Sue Blackmore in *The Meme Machine*). I spent a few years trying (and failing) to operationalize the concept of memes but, like most really dangerous ideas, what I read about cultural evolution has never gone away, and sits somewhere in my head, colouring much of the way I think about education. Thus I shall, perhaps in the hope of catharsis, relate some of these ideas here.

Caveat: It's easy to cherry-pick bits of evidence to support claims in education; in some respects it's superficially true that 'you can prove anything with facts' – if you're not too fussy about which 'facts' you include, or their quality. I may be accused of this a bit, for while I endeavour to give an accurate sketch of the psychological evidence relevant to cultural evolution and human cognition, I speculate a fair bit about how this might apply to education. However, I hope the reader will find this discussion of some of the research arising from evolutionary and cognitive psychology avoids entirely devolving into 'instinct and blind prejudice' on my part. If the reader is especially charitable, they might even find it provides a not-entirely-uninteresting perspective for thinking about the trivium.

A Brief Natural History of Education

Evolutionary psychologists, such as Richard Byrne and Andrew Whiten, Leda Cosmides and John Tooby, have started to piece together the fascinating story of how we evolved our intelligence and capacity for culture. The ability to learn, in the most basic stimulus–response or operant forms, is widespread in the animal kingdom. However, it is the ability to transcend the painful and uncertain process of learning via individual discovery through trial and error that sets us apart. Many other animals appear able to learn from one another to varying degrees, and a few even appear to teach each other some good tricks (adaptive behaviours), but human beings are deeply brilliant at it. Education, in its broadest sense, is what makes Homo sapiens such a unique kind of animal.

Most social animals, even invertebrates, are attracted to the presence and behaviour of members of the same species. This requires very little flexibility in intelligence or capacity to socially learn, but still allows these animals to exploit food resources or discover good nesting sites. However, many non-human animals also appear genuinely capable of social learning. Difficult cognitive tricks like imitation – for example, birds imitating a local 'dialect' of song – and emulation – for example, tool use in chimpanzees – lie at the heart of this ability. These can form 'traditions', observed in primates and some other species of mammals, birds and even fish. In this sense, a 'tradition' is a durable characteristic of a group of individual animals which is created and sustained through repeated social learning.

Beyond passing on and sustaining a clever trick or two, to what extent do other animals possess culture? Some anthropologists, like Miriam Haidle et al. (2015: 55), suggest that a basic cultural capacity might be recognized where there exists a diversity of traditions within a social group. The great apes appear to exhibit this diversity of tradition – to a lesser degree, perhaps so too do some other primates and cetaceans. However, even the most advanced forms of non-human animal culture lack a key feature of human culture: a 'cumulative culture', where more complex cultural forms are built upon existing ones. The cultural traditions of chimpanzees, for instance, have no examples of making and using one tool to shape a second. In the absence of a few (hotly debated) exceptions, only hominids appear to have evolved this ability.

Haidle et al. (2015) attempt to summarize our current understanding of the evolution of cultural capacity in pre-human species of hominid. From the oldest known flaked stone tool (fashioned some 2.6 million years ago) onwards, there's evidence of the emergence of this cumulative culture. Stone napping, for example, involves second-order tools – a hammerstone used to create sharp flakes for cutting. The tools of hominids also started to transcend a single, fixed purpose (unlike those of chimpanzees) and started to gain a variety of functional options.

Two million years ago, evidence of 'industry' supported the production of these tools, with raw materials being shipped over kilometres and the production of cutting tools in quantities far in excess of what may have been immediately needed. The emergence of modular cultural capacity – the ability to combine a variety of tools to construct new tools – led to marvels of technological innovation. For example, archaeologists have found wooden spears made around 300,000 years ago which needed several tools to construct, which in turn required other tools to create those tools. By 70,000 years ago, the hafting of stone tools involved using a compound adhesive made from resin, ochre powder and possibly beeswax. Around this time, tools begin to complement each other in synergistic ways, like a needle and thread or a bow and arrow.

The construction of these tools requires the social transmission of formal information. It is not simply the components involved, but information about the whole system that needs to be communicated; how the different components will eventually be used together. About 40,000 years ago, these concrete and instrumental cultural tools were joined by notional ones; ways to represent the objects of myth and states of mind. These abstract objects of the mind required social representations and complex language in order to be shared; the signs and semiotics which form what many people think of as 'culture'.

This notional cultural capacity allowed the representation of number. Simple tallies made by carving notches in wood or bone may have emerged around the same time as this ability. By around 6,000 years ago, small clay tokens strung like beads on a string appear to have been used by people in what is now Iran. Around 5,200 years ago, people started to invent systems for representing language through graphical symbols, with the first true alphabet emerging some 3,000 years ago. Based on pre-existing ideographic and mnemonic forms of conveying information, the technology of writing started to take off and cultural evolution went into overdrive!

What's incredible is how fast cultural evolution takes off once it starts to accumulate in this way. It all happened so quickly: from the slow collection of cultural tricks over tens of thousands of years, writing emerged and we reached our modern era in a very short space of time. Over a mere few thousand years, we have seen an ever-accelerating pace in our cultural evolution.

The 3,000-year-old Bronze Age Phoenician alphabet, itself probably derived from Egyptian hieroglyphics, was borrowed by the ancient Greeks to record their stories and philosophies. In turn, the Greek alphabet likely formed the basis of the Latin script which travelled with the Romans across Europe and beyond a couple of thousand years ago. Literacy declined in Europe after the collapse of the Roman Empire, but some of what was thought and said by the ancients was saved by Arabic scholars and filtered back into the West during the Renaissance. Writing was initially very expensive. Clay tablets, parchment and vellum were all either expensive to produce or in limited supply. Made from pulped wood or rags, cheap paper was produced, then the first printing press began just over 500 years ago. Ideas begin to circulate more quickly through books, newspapers and pamphlets, sparking the Enlightenment and the scientific revolution.

By the mid-20th century, ideas that had been circulating for centuries regarding a general counting machine gave birth to the computer. Ideas for networking computers together evolved swiftly in the 1960s and 1970s, leading to a standardized Internet Protocol in the early 1980s. The early 1990s saw the advent of the World Wide Web. By the late 1990s the growth of the internet was exponential. The new century saw mobile phones being able to send text messages, then blogging, Facebook, Twitter and other social media. By 2011, social media had become accessible from almost anywhere on Earth.

The philosopher Daniel Dennett (1995: 354) suggests that Darwinian evolution depends upon a high fidelity of transmission. If information suffers too many copying errors, good tricks can be lost from the population as quickly as they might appear. At some point the accuracy with which cultural information was able to be passed on seems to have crossed some sort of threshold, allowing cultural evolution to take off. Chimpanzees might discover a good foraging trick and (if by fortune it is directly observed and imitated), it might be passed on to their troop, but it appears they lack the cognitive architecture required for cumulative culture. Early hominids may have been able to accumulate culture, but without the technology to represent and store these ideas, they could swiftly become lost through accident or poor communication.

This ability to code and decode notional culture allows us to become time travellers within the realm of ideas. Writing allows us to reach across the sands of time to the occasional diamonds that emerged from the dust. According to psychologist Susan Blackmore, it allowed some 'good, useful, true, or beautiful' ideas to travel across this brief period of written history and survive to this day (Blackmore, 2007: 4). Indeed, in the information age, our ability to store and communicate notional culture appears almost unlimited. I say almost unlimited, for there is perhaps one pretty fundamental limitation: our brains are basically the same as those of Upper Palaeolithic humans.

Preparing Young People for the Future with Brains from the Stone Age

In *Educating the Evolved Mind*, David Geary (2007) argues for a distinction between two types of knowledge and ability: those that are biologically primary and emerge instinctively by virtue of our evolved cognitive structures, and those that are biologically secondary and exclusively cultural, acquired through formal or informal instruction or training. Evolution through natural selection has built brains that eagerly and rapidly learn the sorts of things which benefited our capability to survive and reproduce.

These primary forms of knowledge and ability are not inflexible, but they readily process quite restricted classes of information. Geary divides these biologically primary domains into folk psychology (interest in people), folk biology (interest in living things) and folk physics (interest in inanimate objects), and suggests that we have a motivational bias towards learning within these primary domains (e.g. peer interaction, play hunting of other species, play and exploration of the physical environment)(Geary, 2007: 13). So adaptive were these kinds of knowledge, that over time we evolved the ability to create symbolic representations of experiences and techniques like storytelling to communicate these experiences.

Geary also points out that children's inherent motivational bias to adapt folk knowledge to the local social environment will often conflict with the need to engage in activities that will result in secondary learning: interacting with your friendship group will always feel more important and fun than doing homework. Another reason why children may struggle with motivation in school is that the cognitive resources we use to learn are well adapted for biologically primary knowledge, but have been co-opted (the term evolutionary psychologists use is 'exapted') for the purposes of learning secondary (purely cultural) knowledge. Learning to read or learning mathematics are not 'natural' human activities – in the sense that these technologies have been around for such a short time that evolution through natural selection hasn't had much of a chance to shape our brains to learn them as easily as we learn 'folk knowledge'. As a result, such activities are typically much more difficult and take more effort.

A famous illustration of the contrast between how readily we process information that is aligned to folk knowledge (which our brains are adapted for) compared to how difficult we find the sort of formal or abstract information typical of secondary knowledge is the Wason card test.

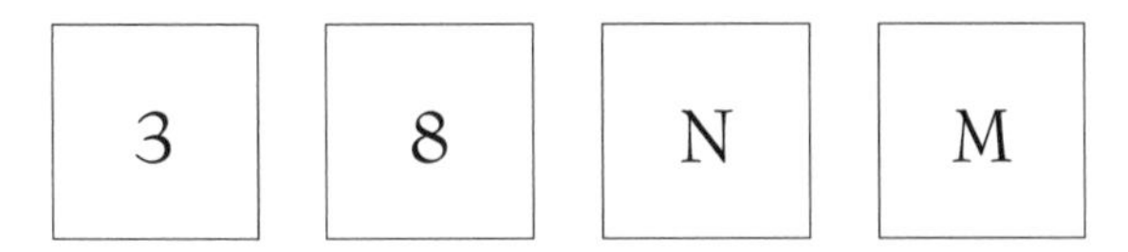

Fig. 1: Abstract version

The card test, originally developed by Peter Wason as a test of deductive reasoning, goes like this. Four cards are placed on a table. Each card has a number on one side and a letter on the other. The cards are shown in the figure above. The question is: Which card(s) must you turn over in order to test the claim that if a card has a 3 on one side, then its opposite side has the letter M?

Many people find this task confusing and difficult, often give the wrong answer (the correct answer is 3 and N), and don't always see why those cards are the correct answer. Leda Cosmides and John Tooby (1992: 182) adapted this task to put it into a context involving policing a social rule, essentially the detection of cheating. To illustrate the idea, consider the scenario of trying to catch underage drinkers. Now, each card has a person's age on one side and a beverage on the back. The question is: Which card(s) must you turn over to check that, if someone is drinking alcohol, they must be at least 18 years old?

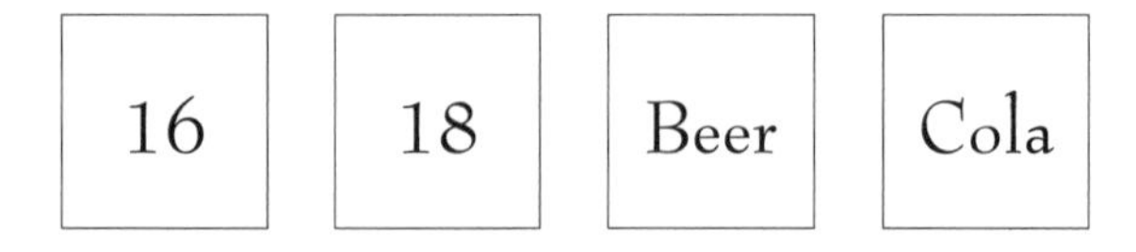

Fig. 2: Drinking age version

It's the same problem, but this time the right answer is much more intuitive (16 and Beer) and many more people solve this version correctly. The explanation for this difference in our ability to solve the card test is that the detection of social cheating was extremely important during our evolutionary history, according to Byrne and Whiten's (1988) Machiavellian intelligence hypothesis, so our brains have adapted to rapidly and easily process information in this form, compared to the abstract original version. We don't care if the 18-year-old is drinking cola or how old the person drinking cola might be; we want to test if anyone is cheating (drinking underage).

Humans have very recently, in evolutionary terms, started to significantly accumulate biologically secondary knowledge (science, mathematics, art, literature, engineering, computing, etc.). Geary suggests that these cultural advances have resulted in an ever-growing gap between folk knowledge (easy and intuitive) and this growing cultural knowledge base (more difficult to learn) needed for living in society, and that schools emerged in societies to close the gap between the two.

The philosopher and psychologist Peter Carruthers suggests that human working memory is shared by at least other primates, and likely other mammals as well. There's some evidence to suggest that monkeys and horses have a memory span of 3–4 items, similar to humans, and that other primates have pure retention abilities similar to those of humans. There's even evidence that other primates may have superior aspects of working memory compared to humans. For example, chimpanzees appear to have an incredible visual memory, and on masking tasks (where numerals are flashed up on a screen and almost immediately covered up) have shown the ability to memorize long sequences in the blink of an eye, far exceeding human ability.

Non-human animals have also shown a capacity for anticipating and planning for the future. An amusing example of this ability to plan was reported in *New Scientist* in 2009 (Gedes, 2009). Santino, a 30-year-old chimpanzee at Furuvik Zoo in Sweden, was observed deliberately fashioning and storing discs of concrete to later throw at tourists. According to Martin et al. (2014), chimpanzees may also even have a better grasp of competitive strategy than humans. In a two-player video game, players had to choose between left and right squares on a touch-screen panel, while not being able to see their opponent's choice. A player won (apple cubes for the chimpanzees; money for the humans) if they both selected the same panel; the other player won if they did not. Martin analysed the results and found that the chimpanzees' choices were closer to the ideal solution predicted by equilibrium game theory than human choices.

However, in a couple of respects, human working memory appears superior to that of other animals. First, our executive functioning, a hypothesized capacity for things like problem-solving, reasoning, planning and organization, inhibiting action (or speech) within context-appropriate norms and managing attention control (among other things). Second, our superior linguistic ability, which (among other things), allows us to use 'inner speech' to help hold and manipulate information in memory. It may also be the case that we are able to make frequent, task-independent use of our working memory, ruminating and letting our mind wander in a way that other animals cannot do. However, our ability to process visual-spatial information and draw on long-term memory to help us solve problems and make plans for the future appears to be shared with other primates, and probably many other mammals as well.

The problem for teachers is that working memory is well adapted to processing the sorts of information and solving the sorts of problem related to biologically primary knowledge. Humans appear to have exapted this cognitive resource to deal with biologically secondary knowledge acquisition – and, as a result, we find such learning difficult.

Psychologists often use the term 'schema' (pl. schemata) when talking about the encoding and retrieval of information from our long-term memory. First introduced by psychologists such as Piaget and Bartlett, a schema can be thought of as an organized framework representing some aspect of the world and a system of organizing that information. The classic example used frequently in psychology is going to a restaurant (I've no idea why; perhaps psychologists can't cook). The schema for getting a table, ordering food and drink, and paying for the meal, makes visiting a new restaurant for the first time, even in another country, a pretty straightforward process, as we deal with new situations by linking them to things we've encountered in the past. Most of the time we can rely on pre-existing schemata as a heuristic, or rule of thumb: it requires little thought and acts like a cognitive 'shortcut' when dealing with new information.

Schemata provide a quick and painless way to deal with new information and allow us to cope with complex changes in the environment or social situation by quickly drawing on our prior experiences. They can also get in the way when learning. Schemata readily form around biologically primary knowledge and act as rough-and-ready rules, intuitive but also often stereotyped or based on misconceptions. When drawing upon schemata we make minimal use of working memory – it simply doesn't need very much conscious reasoning. Daniel Kahneman, in *Thinking, Fast and Slow* (2011), describes this as 'system 1 thinking': fast, effortless, based on emotions and stereotypes, and usually subconscious. As a result, it leaves decision-making open to a wide variety of cognitive biases. These biases represent essential ways in which humans are irrational in their thinking and decision-making, but probably emerged because they were in some way adaptive in our evolutionary past (e.g. Geary (2007: 4) suggests such cognitive biases form the basis of primary 'folk knowledge'). Many examples of these biases and the ways in which these may influence the decisions made in schools are discussed in David Didau's book, *What if Everything You Knew about Education was Wrong?*

Jean Piaget believed learning occurred when there was a mismatch between a schema held in mind and feedback from the environment (e.g. what would happen if you tried to use the restaurant schema to get a drink in a British pub?). The mismatch, he argued, created a sense of discomfort – cognitive conflict – which was resolved by the modification of the schema to accommodate the new information. However, subsequent research suggests that schemata are highly resistant to change, and it seems that we are more likely to simply disregard information which doesn't accord with a schema rather than change it. Along with memory, there's evidence that schemata influence our attention, our perceptions and our interpretations of events, and thus can lead us to overlook information which contradicts our prior beliefs and expectations.

I think there is also a question about whether schemas are actually modified at all, or whether newly acquired schemas merely sit alongside the old ones. In this case the schema used in a particular situation depends upon which version of it is activated; subtle differences in the context, and the frequency with which a particular schema is used, may cause one schema to come to mind or a similar alternative one. This can make life difficult for teachers and their students. For example, you can teach a Year 8 student all about photosynthesis, that the carbon which forms the basis of wood comes from carbon dioxide absorbed from the air; however, when asked, 'Where does the wood of a tree come from?' the unusual context of the question doesn't activate the new schema and an older 'folk biology' schema may be activated instead (so the child says 'the soil', for example).

Kahneman contrasts this fast 'schematic' processing with system 2 thinking, which is slow, effortful, logical and conscious. We can relate this to what's happening when working memory becomes heavily involved in the processing of new information. It's hard and we don't especially enjoy it. The brain has evolved to make efficient use of schemata (which form most readily around the 'folk knowledge' needed to survive and reproduce) and when a schema doesn't fit we possess only limited capacity for conscious problem-solving. To quote psychologist Daniel Willingham, 'Your brain serves many purposes, and thinking is not the one it serves best' (Willingham, 2009: 4).

The psychologist John Sweller calls this 'cognitive load' (Sweller, 1994). Several things can add to this load on working memory, he suggests. One source is the intrinsic load imposed by the new information; the difficulty imposed by the learning task itself. For an example of how context can affect the intrinsic difficulty of a task, compare the original Wason card test to the Cosmides and Tooby example. The social cheating version is intrinsically easier than the abstract version, perhaps because our brains have evolved to rapidly process the former type of problem. A second source is the extraneous load; the difficulty imposed by the way the information is presented. A simple example is where a teacher presents a diagram on a whiteboard which has separate labels alongside (as opposed to labels within the diagram itself). The need to constantly switch attention (from the diagram to the label and back), remember the text, and link that back to its role within the diagram creates a load on working memory which isn't especially helpful or useful. Where the cognitive load imposed by a learning task outstrips an individual's fairly limited working memory capacity, we'd expect very little learning to take place.

From this, a teacher might infer that by reducing intrinsic difficulty (e.g. putting learning within a familiar context) and extraneous load (e.g. by minimizing distractions or the need for attention switching) children will learn more effectively, but it turns out to be more complicated than this. Robert Bjork suggests that merely speeding up the rate of knowledge acquisition during a lesson may fail to support long-term retention of that knowledge and the ability to transfer that knowledge to new contexts. He suggests that effective learning requires the presence of 'desirable difficulties'; providing intermittent, rather than immediate, feedback and delayed retrieval practice (e.g. through frequent quizzes) rather than one-off, immediate assessments of learning (e.g. through student presentations). Sweller's theory encompassed this idea with a final form of cognitive load, germane load, which represents the opportunity to construct and automate the new information as a schema.

There has been considerable debate relating to the inclusion of germane load. One problem is that it is very difficult to objectively say whether an aspect of a learning task will be extraneous or germane. This ambiguity risks making the theory unfalsifiable, as any experimental effect that benefited learning can be labelled, post hoc, as germane load, while anything that appears to be detrimental to learning can be labelled extraneous. The debate is far from settled, but to my mind germane load relates to (and shares some of the same problems as) Craik and Lockhart's 'levels of processing effect' (Craik and Lockhart, 1972). They suggested that the strength of long-term memory was dependent upon the 'depth of processing' used during the encoding of the material. Shallow processing (e.g. Structural – attending to what words or letters look like) leads to short memory traces, while deeper processing (e.g. Phonemic – attending to the sounds of a word) leads to slightly longer traces, and the deepest processing (e.g. Semantic – attending to what the words mean) leads to the longest memory traces.

This was tested in a famous experiment by Craik and Tulving (1975) in which participants answered a series of yes/no questions. At the shallowest level of processing, participants merely had to answer a question about a word's appearance – for example, whether it appeared in capital letters. A deeper level of processing was required for questions relating to the auditory qualities of the word (for example, whether the word rhymed with 'pencil'). Finally, the deepest level of processing was provided by questions that related to the semantic properties of the word (for example, whether the word would fit into the context of a sentence). As predicted, items which required participants to answer semantic-level questions tended to be recalled better than those requiring more superficial processing.

The concept of germane load has some utility when talking about teaching. For example, many teachers will use a word search involving the key terms in a lesson, in the hope that the activity will help consolidate those terms for future use. However, it seems clear that such activities are likely aimed at the wrong level of processing – they lack germane load. It's possible to make word search puzzles quite difficult to complete (by having some words run backwards, for instance), but the task is essentially a 'structural' one, requiring no thought about the meanings of the words. On the other hand, if a teacher wants to have a puzzle element to a lesson, a crossword with clues related to the definitions of each word might be more effective. In essence, the effortful thought required in a lesson needs to be aimed at the semantic level to increase the chances that knowledge is retained.

Some questions a teacher might consider based on cognitive load theory: How can we minimize extraneous load on working memory as much as possible? What will students be thinking about – how can we focus effortful thought on what we want them to learn? Are there social/environmental distractors which can be reduced? Is there irrelevant information/images which can be trimmed to improve that focus?

Can we moderate intrinsic load as a way of raising the challenge of a lesson or (conversely) increasing student ability to access material? How concrete/abstract is the information? How much prior knowledge do students have already? How many ideas are we asking them to 'juggle' at once? How challenging is the reading age of material? Can we link an image directly to the concept being explained, to provide a visual mode that can be processed alongside a verbal explanation? When dealing with difficult new concepts or processes, how might we use worked examples to potentially reduce the load on working memory?

How can we increase the germane load (the 'desirable difficulties') of a lesson? How much focused and effortful thought is required to complete the given activity? Are there opportunities to apply the new knowledge/processes to a range of examples? How will we allow students to practise over an extended period of time? How will students use the new knowledge to support future learning? To what extent is the lesson focused on the deeper, semantic level of the material?

Grammar

As mentioned earlier, the biologically secondary knowledge which drives our cumulative culture is frequently learned slowly and with difficulty, and almost always requires conscious cognitive effort. However, with practice (over time and across a wide variety of contexts) this secondary cultural knowledge can become more automated as schema. We successfully do this throughout our lives. For example, as your eyes flick across this sentence, you are effortlessly decoding it; learning to drive and navigating traffic was difficult to begin with, but after some time you can drive home and not remember the journey you have just made. It becomes automatic.

As biologically secondary schemata become automated, less cognitive load is imposed when learning new material that relies upon them – for example, a physicist can read an article on dark matter and the familiarity of terms such as 'gravitational lensing', 'cosmic microwave background', 'WIMPs' and so on allows them to quickly comprehend the material and later recall the new information it contained, whereas if you are unfamiliar with the terms and ideas, the demands of the task can quickly overload your limited processing ability and you will likely gain very little from the exercise.

With respect to the trivium, this implies the importance of what Martin Robinson describes as grammar; the idea of foundational knowledge that provides the basis for future learning. The key methods for coding and decoding biologically secondary knowledge, reading and mathematics, or the 'cultural capital' required to share in the broader cultural life of society, are a vital part of education (and perhaps what it means to be 'educated'). It forms the underpinning to that quintessentially human wonder, cumulative culture, which (if he'll forgive me putting words in his mouth) Martin might prefer to describe using Michael Oakeshott's idea of an initiation into 'the conversation of mankind' (Robinson, 2015).

To achieve this cumulative culture requires a robust inheritance of ideas in order to take off; otherwise learned adaptive behaviours get lost as quickly as they might arise. However, a reliable form of cultural transmission is necessary, but not sufficient, for cultural evolution to take place: there must also be variation among these cultural ideas, and some form of selection operating upon them.

Dialectic

What acts as the selective environment for ideas? Why do some ideas survive for hundreds, sometimes thousands, of years, whereas others quickly disappear? In our evolutionary past, it was likely the same environment selecting our culture as the one selecting our genes; those practices and habits which aided our survival and reproduction could be passed on to offspring along with the genes which helped us adapt to our environment.

Later, as we began to record our notional culture in writing, the sheer effort and cost in reproducing texts likely formed a selective environment for those ideas. But the advent of cheaper methods to reproduce information, the concordant expansion of literacy and, not least, the development of information and communication technology has made it possible for ideas to be transmitted and survive, regardless of their 'adaptive value' in terms of the natural selection of genes. Susan Blackmore, in *The Meme Machine* (1999), suggests that cultural evolution has taken on a 'life' of its own, entirely independent of biological evolution. However, for evolution to take place there still has to be an element of selection – not all ideas can survive and be passed on.

There are many informal ways in which cultural ideas might get selected; one book may be better written, more entertaining or simply more popular and sell better than others. Some songs may be 'catchy' or inspire stronger emotions than others. Some political ideas may resonate with the electorate (or simply hook on to the prevailing prejudices of the times) better than others.

One example of a more formal selective environment for ideas is science. Science isn't merely a collection of 'facts' or an accumulation of evidence: instead, it is a crucible for cultural ideas. To get passed on or widely distributed, a scientific idea has to survive a process of critical dialectic; questioning and challenge by peers and the gauntlet of empirical testing. Of course, shoddy ideas sometimes slip through this process and scientists, like everyone else, are capable of cheating, but over time science acts as a selective pressure on ideas – weeding out the ones that fail the crucible and propagating the ones that survive.

Another example of more formal selection acting upon cultural ideas relates directly to education: the idea of a national curriculum or 'core knowledge' forming the basis of the grammar taught in schools. Some elements of this are relatively uncontroversial – the framework for coding and decoding, and some basic elements of literacy and numeracy. However, one does not have to look hard to see where this state form of selection becomes contentious. Whether it is arguments about what books should form part of GCSE English, or which elements of history should be taught in primary schools, teachers are often instinctively wary about politicians selecting the elements of culture which will form the basis of future learning. On the other hand, the idea that teachers should select entirely for themselves what elements of culture should be taught is equally problematic. We all have different ideas about what is important for children to learn. Without any kind of common framework, this could easily lead to inequality: for example, children from less affluent backgrounds could be denied the exposure to cultural ideas afforded to children in wealthier families.

One answer to this has been the suggestion that children select their own curriculum. However, this may represent an even worse solution to the problem of centralized state control and libertarian autonomy for teachers. Some people, such as Sugata Mitra, suggest that children can readily self-organize biologically secondary knowledge for themselves (armed only with a computer and access to the internet) – but while this may be true for some children, it is highly unlikely to be true for the vast majority. Geary (2007: 9) suggests that we are highly motivated to engage in the kind of learning that is suited for developing biologically primary knowledge, implying that children left to their own devices would likely struggle with the kind of learning needed for biologically secondary knowledge.

Even where a teacher actively facilitates a curriculum chosen by students, the capacity for inequality is still a problem. For example, children who benefit from the encouragement of educated parents may choose to study aspects of secondary culture that children without these advantages may not even know exists.

In the tradition of the trivium, I suspect the solution lies in the dialectic tension between these competing interests. Children will learn secondary knowledge more easily if they have some prior knowledge and personal interest in a topic, but I'd argue that somewhere between a democratic debate and teacher or school discretion there are some diamonds among the dust which should be selected for them, because children would be better able to participate in our society from having them put in their way.

Rhetoric

The last element required for cultural evolution is some form of variation. It is not enough that ideas are simply replicated from one generation to the next. For cumulative culture to actually accumulate, variations and novel ideas must be constantly added to the mix. We see further by standing upon the shoulders of giants, but our task as educators is not only to encourage children to understand the works of those giants, but also to see further. Martin's ideas about rhetoric might best fit this aspect of cultural evolution.

There exists, I suspect, a rather romanticized view of children's creativity which is rather at odds with observations from psychology. To pick an example, the role play of younger children tends to be highly gender-schematized. Using Geary's ideas, this is understandable. Implicitly acquired biologically primary knowledge tends towards an 'intuitive' understanding (or folk knowledge) of how to engage in social interactions with other members of our species. Often despite the best intentions of parents, who may consciously encourage non-gender-specific toys and activities, children rapidly acquire stereotypic ideas about gender identity and reflect these (often quite rigidly) in their play.

Young children naturally possess a relatively limited set of schemata, and thus their ability to be creative (to combine schemata from different domains to generate interesting variations) is also fairly limited. What probably impresses us as adults is the uninhibited way children make productions based on these limited schemata. Princesses are painted, doctors and nurses are role played, cardboard robots are constructed without embarrassment, and these unselected productions are usually (and quite naturally) rewarded by praise and attention.

However, centuries of cumulative culture have taken us beyond these stereotyped productions. As we get older we begin to identify more with our peers and, even if our parents still encourage us, our creativity starts to undergo more internal selection before production. Over time we come to understand that the first thoughts that pop into our heads are rarely true expressions of genius, and the nature of our creativity starts to expand and change. The grammar of foundational culture expands the cultural schemata available to us and the dialectic of selection starts to challenge the quality of our rhetoric; the creative performances and productions we share with others.

It's long been fashionable to claim, as Ken Robinson does, that education somehow stifles creativity, but the reverse is much more likely to be the case: look at the sheer cultural variety available to us today – the books, the films, the plays, the games, the food, the clothing, the shoes, the science, the art, the music – compared to what previous generations of humans enjoyed. To add something novel and successful to that cultural variety is no mean feat, yet human beings continue to do so at a rate the world has never seen before. Education doesn't stifle human cultural creativity; it is the very engine which drives it. It is the foundation for that cumulative capacity of culture which makes us uniquely human.

For me, creativity is a chimera (a Greek mythical creature cobbled together from parts of a lion, a goat and a serpent); the ability to exapt an idea from one domain and apply it to another in an interesting way. Like the mutation of genes, I wonder whether most of these creative variations of schema tend to be pretty random and unsuccessful (certainly, many will be unoriginal). Thus the creative products of adults tend to undergo significant internal selection before public performance.

However, it could be argued that knowledge and skill alone cannot account for creativity. Why is it that some people (who are perhaps equally knowledgeable or skilful) appear to be more creative than others? One of the unique features of human cognition is our ability to make frequent, task-independent use of our working memory. We are able to ruminate and let our mind wander in a way that other animals probably do not. Is this a 'creative mode' of human thought?

In Iain M. Bank's Culture novels, the utopian anarchy of the Culture is run by godlike artificial intelligences called 'Minds'. Able to think 'faster than light', these Minds entertain themselves within an 'infinite fun space': universe-level mathematical simulations explored within their own imaginations. Mere humans, with our Stone Age brains possessing limited memory capacity and a processing speed that is very much sub-the speed of light, are incapable of such feats of imagination. However, we are able to retreat into a 'finite fun space'; we have the capacity to engage in a 'play of ideas' which may occasionally give birth to an interesting chimera.

So, while I would argue that formal education in the form of 'high-fidelity cultural transmission' is the engine of human cumulative culture, I'd also argue that it's important that we do not encourage children to see all these ideas as written on tablets of stone. There are aspects of our culture which are abstract and difficult to learn, but after they are well understood they can also be played with somewhat irreverently. Achieving this balance between encouraging children to develop a rigorous internal selection of ideas, yet remain open to playing with these ideas in their 'finite fun space', is a challenge worthy of our profession. I'll end with a quote by Carl Sagan which, I think, summarizes this tension perfectly.

> It seems to me what is called for is an exquisite balance between two conflicting needs: the most skeptical scrutiny of all hypotheses that are served up to us and at the same time a great openness to new ideas. If you are only skeptical, then no new ideas make it through to you. On the other hand, if you are open to the point of gullibility, then you cannot distinguish the useful ideas from the worthless ones. (Quoted in Shermer, 2001: 235)

Some questions a teacher might consider based on ideas about cultural evolution and the trivium:

- Passing on secondary culture isn't merely a process of 'telling'. Great teacher talk frequently makes use of prior assessment to ensure new information builds upon secure knowledge foundations.
- What is the grammar of your subject/the topic you'll be teaching? Even if you are teaching within a fairly constrained curriculum or specification, there are likely to be some concepts, facts or ideas that are more 'foundational' than others. Which are these?
- Great teacher talk also often makes use of analogies, images and worked examples to help moderate cognitive load. Another feature is the use of storytelling or narrative structure; Willingham makes the point that stories have a privileged place in memory. Our brains have adapted to readily recall stories, and he suggests we might use the abstract structure of stories (he suggests causality, conflict, complications and character) within a sequence of learning. How might we exploit this adaptation of memory to help students build firmer foundations of knowledge?
- How do students 'select' which schema to use when tackling questions or problems in lessons? Perhaps, as Geary implies, the more our subject relies upon biologically secondary knowledge, the more readily a student will rely upon a misconception based on their prior 'folk knowledge'.
- Which schema is the student using when asked a question? Do they recognize the correct schema when prompted? Can they see why the incorrect schema doesn't answer the question adequately? This is an important aspect of the selective environment – and perhaps provides a framework for understanding the effectiveness of feedback we provide as teachers.
- So, can we educate for creativity? It is rare that a child has either the domain knowledge(s) or that capacity for selection required to make an inspirational contribution to human culture (though I can think of possible exceptions, such as Mozart). I suspect that confidence in the

foundational grammar of a topic and the ability to engage an internal process of dialectic facilitates the creative performances and productions (rhetoric) we produce. If we genuinely want our students to be creative, then we need to encourage deep knowledge, understanding and skill, and the ability to engage in internal selection of their ideas. Is this a helpful framework for understanding 'metacognition' (what the Sutton Trust-Education Endowment Foundation Toolkit lists as the ability to set goals, monitor and evaluate specific aspects of learning)? By encouraging metacognition, are we sowing the seeds of the internal selection processes needed for the creative play of ideas?

References

Blackmore, Susan (1999) *The Meme Machine*. Oxford: Oxford University Press.

Blackmore, Susan (2007) 'Imitation Makes Us Human'. In Charles Pasternak (ed.), *What Makes Us Human?* Oxford: Oneworld Publications, pp. 1–16.

Byrne, Richard and Whiten, Andrew (1988) *Machiavellian Intelligence*. Oxford: Oxford University Press.

Carruthers, Peter (2015) *The Centered Mind: What The Science Of Working Memory Shows Us About the Nature of Human Thought*. Oxford: Oxford University Press.

Cosmides, Leda and Tooby, John (1992) 'Cognitive Adaptions for Social Exchange'. In Jerome Barkow, Leda Cosmides and John Tooby (eds), *The Adapted Mind: Evolutionary Psychology and the Generation of Culture*. New York: Oxford University Press, pp. 163–228.

Craik, Fergus and Lockhart, Robert (1972) 'Levels of Processing: A Framework for Memory Research', *Journal of Verbal Learning and Verbal Behavior*, 11(6): 671–684.

Craik, Fergus and Tulving, Endel (1975) 'Depth of Processing and the Retention of Words in Episodic Memory', *Journal of Experimental Psychology: General*, 104(3): 268–294.

Dawkins, Richard (1976) *The Selfish Gene*. Oxford: Oxford University Press.

Dennett, Daniel (1995) *Darwin's Dangerous Idea*. London: Penguin.

Didau, David (2015) *What If Everything You Knew About Education Was Wrong?* Carmarthen: Crown House Publishing.

Geary, David C. (2007) 'Educating the Evolved Mind: Conceptual Foundations for an Evolutionary Educational Psychology'. In Jerry S. Carlson and Joel R. Levin (eds), *Educating the Evolved Mind*. Greenwich, CT: Information Age, pp. 1–99.

Gedes, Linda (2009) 'Missile-throwing Chimp Plots Attacks on Tourists', *New Scientist*, 9 March. Available at: https://www.newscientist.com/article/dn16726-missile-throwing-chimp-plots-attacks-on-tourists/.

Haidle, Miriam Noël, Bolus, Michael, Collard, Mark, et al. (2015) 'The Nature of Culture: An Eight-Grade Model for the Evolution and Expansion of Cultural Capacities in Hominins and Other Animals', *Journal of Anthropological Sciences*, 93: 43–70.

Kahneman, Daniel (2011) *Thinking, Fast and Slow*. New York: Farrar, Straus and Giroux.

Lee, Stewart (2010) *How I Escaped my Certain Fate*. London: Faber and Faber.

Martin, Christopher Flynn, Bhui, Rahul, Bossaerts, Peter, et al. (2014) 'Chimpanzee Choice Rates in Competitive Games Match Equilibrium Game Theory Predictions', *Scientific Reports*, 4(5182). DOI:10.1038/srep05182.

Piaget, Jean (1961) 'The Genetic Approach to the Psychology of Thought', *Journal of Educational Psychology*, 52: 275–281.

Robinson, Ken (2006) Do Schools Kill Creativity, *TED Talk*. Available at: https://www.ted.com/talks/ken_robinson_says_schools_kill_creativity?language=en.

Robinson, Martin (2015) 'Voices: An Initiation into the Conversation of Mankind', *Trivium 21c* [blog] (7 March). Available at: https://martinrobborobinson.wordpress.com/2015/03/07/voices-an-initiation-into-the-conversation-of-mankind/.

Shermer, Michael (2001) *The Borderlands of Science: Where Sense Meets Nonsense*. Oxford: Oxford University Press.

Sutton Trust-Education Endowment Foundation (n.d.), Teaching and Learning Toolkit. Available at: https://educationendowmentfoundation.org.uk/evidence/teaching-learning-toolkit/.

Sweller, John (1994) 'Cognitive Load Theory, Learning Difficulty and Instructional Design', *Learning and Instruction*, 4: 295–312.

Sweller, John (2010) 'Element Interactivity and Intrinsic, Extraneous, and Germane Cognitive Load', *Educational Psychology Review*, 22(2): 123–138.

Willingham, Daniel (2009) *Why Don't Students Like School? A Cognitive Scientist Answers Questions about How the Mind Works and What it Means for the Classroom*. San Francisco, CA: Jossey-Bass.

Chapter 8

Dialogue and Dialogic: The Trivium and Bakhtin

Carl Hendrick

This chapter explores how Bakhtin's ideas of 'dialogic', 'carnival' and 'inauthenticity' can inform classroom practice and support the broader ambition of the trivium.

Carl Hendrick is the Head of Learning and Research at Wellington College, in Crowthorne, Berkshire, where he teaches English. He has taught for several years in both the state and independent sectors, and has worked on several cross-sectoral collaborations. His areas of interest are practitioner-led research in schools, Bakhtin and dialogism. In 2014 he established the Wellington Learning and Research Centre. Among the many projects he is leading is a two-year collaboration with the Harvard Graduate School of Education faculty to evaluate student motivation. He is also completing a PhD at King's College London.

It's a curious aspect of education that the thing that we ask students to do the most is often the thing that is the least considered by educators – talking. We will spend weeks planning schemes of work, presentations and lesson plans, but give precious little thought to how we might engender the kind of classroom exchange that will allow students to truly engage with knowledge.

Too often it seems that, in order to satisfy the demands of assessment and data, we privilege the superficiality of certainty over the irresolution of ambiguity, but it is precisely within that liminal space of uncertainty that some of the most productive and fruitful dialogue can often take place.

We are all familiar with the individual aspects of the trivium and their function as constituent parts of the whole, but the thread that stitches them together is *dialogue*. However, how often can we claim that this dialogue is truly 'dialogic' – and what does that even mean? It's helpful to parse out some of these terms at the outset, and then begin to think about ways we can harness them in the classroom.

Broadly speaking, we can think of two modes of class discourse: monologic and dialogic. Monologic refers to the kind of interaction that is essentially one-way traffic, characterized by very fixed positions of authority, and sometimes closed in nature, whereas dialogic refers to an exchange that embraces difference, celebrates the voice of the other, and seeks to open up meaning rather than limit it.

However, I want to argue that one crucial aspect of the contemporary dialogic classroom that is often neglected is the role of knowledge, and that contemporary education has prioritized thinking skills over thinking itself – which needs knowledge in order to be of any use at all.

Of course, it's tempting to think that these two positions nicely fall along partisan lines of traditional and progressive – but this is not so. Indeed, these modes can be interchangeable, and even dependent on one another. So while we are all au fait with the term 'dialogue', we are perhaps less so with the term 'dialogic' or even 'dialogism', a term coined by an obscure Russian philosopher called Mikhail Bakhtin. It is his work that I want to focus on, to outline a way that we might think more deeply about classroom talk.

In *Trivium 21c* Martin Robinson wrote that: 'Mikhail Bakhtin used the word 'dialogic' to describe a conversation that uses a process of exchange to listen and empathize with, but not necessarily agree' (Robinson, 2013: 130). Bakhtin did not believe it was necessary for synthesis and agreement. Indeed, if a classroom is to be a truly free place for exchange of views and open for all in which to learn then the idea of closing a dialectic down through 'synthesis', might be an outcome that leaves some to silence their thoughts. How can dialectic be a process that doesn't just mean that the majority or, indeed the teacher, is the only source of 'truth'? Can we agree to disagree?

'Neither a First nor Last Word': Who is Mikhail Bakhtin?

Few thinkers have presented as much of a challenge to the fields of literature, linguistics and the social sciences as Mikhail Bakhtin (1895–1975). This is due in no small part to the fact that his work fiercely resists any classification, and is by its very nature very difficult to categorize into any cohesive system of thought. Indeed, there is still much debate as to whether his work is that of a literary scholar, a linguist, a philosopher or a social anthropologist, although some biographers claim that the classification he was most comfortable with was a philosophical anthropologist.

An opponent of canons, he was an individual who was oblique both in his writings and his personal correspondence, of which there is precious little. Much of his writings are fragmented or even lost altogether – there is a very real sense that his work is not meant to be 'read' at all, insofar as he made his work very obtuse and even destroyed much of it himself. Relatively unknown for the majority of his life, he gained a cult status among academics in the 1960s, both in his native Russia and Europe, as his work was appropriated by new schools of thought. Many who met him during this period describe him as a mercurial and highly enigmatic figure who had a measurable impact on their lives and who displayed an almost sage-like appreciation of the human condition.

Much of Bakhtinian thought on education comes from writing that is not specifically about education, but which – when appropriated into the classroom – provides a rich seam of thought relating to not only contemporary classroom dialogue but also, I claim, the impact of recent technological developments. The title of one lost manuscript gives a tantalizing view of what Bakhtin might have written directly about education: The Novel of Education and Its Significance in the History of Realism. This work was sent to the publisher in 1938, only to be destroyed in the German invasion, and left Bakhtin with only the preparatory material. He had been a schoolteacher, before going on to write ground-breaking criticism on the work of Dostoevsky, Freud and Marx. Through his criticism of these works, he began to flesh out ideas that would have wider social and anthropological implications.

There is relatively little biographical information on him, and then, as Rachel Pollard (2008: 2) notes, there is the question of 'which Bakhtin to critically engage with, as there is no central or definitive interpretation of his work'. However, despite the fact that in a contemporary sense he is very much a shadowy figure, in his own lifetime it seems he was very much available. One critic, Matusov, writes that, according to former students, Bakhtin was:

> … a very charismatic, knowledgeable, and enthusiastic teacher, Bakhtin's classes were very popular and crowded with students who wanted to hear his lectures even though they were not formally enrolled in his classes. Often, even faculty members attended his classes. (Matusov, 2004: 4)

At the heart of Bakhtin's work is the notion of the dialogic or the 'interconnectedness' of things. It is a concept that is counterintuitive (in the sense that it promotes the blending of many voices, but not unity). There is also a certain altruistic spirit associated with the authentic dialogic exchange. Indeed, Hilary Putnam (1992: 78) beautifully refers to dialogism as 'a conversation with many voices rather than as a contest with winners and losers'. Bakhtin wrote on subjects as diverse as literature, linguistics and sociology, and so his ideas applied to education in that respect are always tangential, always 'in dialogue' with the practice of pedagogy.

One of the real challenges, and indeed positives, in applying his ideas to the contemporary classroom is that they are completely at odds with the current preoccupation with classification and measurability. Bakhtin would have perhaps regarded the current culture of fixed targets and measurement as very un-dialogic insofar as it represents a 'closing off' of meaning, and of potential dialogue.

For proponents of the Trivium, this approach of enacting an ongoing conversation as opposed to a closed 'truth' is perhaps best explored in the Socratic dialectic technique of *dissoi logoi* as outlined by Martin Robinson:

> By studying two or more texts alongside one another a student might want to agree with one more than the other. Don't let them. The dissoi logoi is a dialogue that presents both sides as carrying equal weight and therefore being equally true. It opens up debate rather than closes it down. It is 'inductive' rather than 'deductive.' (Robinson, 2014a)

This particular approach would have greatly appealed to Bakhtin, who invented many wonderful words to explain his core concepts. Possibly his most central idea is the notion of 'unfinalizability', or the ambiguity of meaning. He wrote:

> There is neither a first nor last word and there are no limits to the dialogic context (it extends into the boundless past and the boundless future). Even past meanings, that is, those born in the dialogue of past centuries, can never be stable (finalized, ended once and for all) – they will always change (be renewed) in the process of subsequent, future development of the dialogue. (Bakhtin, 1986: 170)

It is precisely in this somewhat counterintuitive concept that Bakhtin offers his most powerful potential and affords a radically new way of viewing the creation of knowledge and meaning, and by extension a more holistic development of the learner. The phrase 'the boundless past and the boundless future' has particular resonance in regards to the kinds of exchanges that the trivium model affords and, indeed, the kinds of change created by the internet, and the way in which the challenge of how to obtain information has now been subsumed by the challenge of what to do with the abundance of it.

I feel it instructive at this point to look more closely at some of his central concepts and how they might enable us to think about the trivium – and specifically classroom talk – in a new way.

Dialogue vs Monologue

One of the most interesting claims that Bakhtin makes about literature is that Dostoevsky is one of the few writers worth reading because you cannot detect the writer's authorial presence in his work: the characters speak for themselves and incorporate a range of other voices from the past, present and future. He asserts that the novel is a truly revolutionary art form because of this very aspect, as opposed to the more traditional forms of writing, such as epic poetry, that are very fixed in terms of form and scope (see Bakhtin, 1981).

We can consider Bakhtin's work as being characterized by three major concepts; prosaics, dialogue and unfinalizability. In true Bakhtinian style, these three terms are interrelated and continuously speak to each other. His theory of prosaics centres on theories about the novel, and covers a wide and varied range of material from the Epic to Rabelais, but it is in the polyphonic nature of Dostoevsky's work that Bakhtin locates the essence of dialogue insofar as he sees a text as something featuring voices that 'speak' for themselves without any authorial presence.

For Bakhtin, to be in that dialogical space is itself a mode of being. He writes:

> Everything in Dostoevsky's novels gravitates toward the dialogue, toward dialogical opposition, as the centre point. Everything else is the means, the dialogue is the end. One voice alone concludes nothing and decides nothing. Two voices is minimum for life, the minimum for existence. (Bakhtin, 1984: 213)

An important point to establish straight away then is the notion that a dialogic interaction is not merely a vehicle towards a predefined goal but rather a means of becoming in and of itself. Another important distinction at this point is between a dialogic interaction and a dialectical one which for Bakhtin was a form of shifting the goalposts and arriving at a 'finalized' synthesis.

The term dialogic then essentially refers to a process of becoming through dialogue, of entering into an 'unfinalized' arena where there is a plenitude of meaning, an endless labyrinth of possibilities where there is no one closed endpoint.

So it is perhaps helpful to think of a dialogic mode of discussion in contrast with the more closed 'monologic' mode. For Bakhtin, a monologic exchange can be one that has a certain set of fixed parameters, that is often antithetical to formative dialogue and the 'opening up' of meaning. He writes:

> Monologue is finalized and deaf to the other's response, does not expect it and does not acknowledge in it any decisive force. Monologue manages without the other, and therefore to some degree materializes all reality. Monologue pretends to be the ultimate word. It closes down the represented world and represented persons. (Bakhtin, 1984: 292–293)

Now, at this point it is tempting to think about these ideas in terms of the traditional/progressive axis but, as the trivium model has shown, these modes need not be in opposition to each other. The monologic expression can be part of a dialogic interaction; it just requires certain contingent factors. Bakhtin goes on to make the claim that any utterance, even a monologic one, is ultimately within some form of dialogue itself – in the sense that it is both reactionary and anticipatory; it is both answering a previous utterance on the subject and anticipating future voices. However, the element that distinguishes it from previous ones is that it may not be in the spirit of true dialogic interaction, and therefore does not afford the same emancipatory possibility. In *Speech Genres* he writes:

> However monological the utterance may be (for example, a scientific or philosophical treatise), however much it may concentrate on its own object, it cannot but be, in some measure, a response to what has already been said about the given topic, on the given issue, even though this responsiveness may not have assumed a clear-cut external expression. After all, our thought itself – philosophical, scientific, and artistic – is born in the process of interaction and struggle with others' thought. (Bakhtin, 1986: 92)

So the monologue can itself be placed in a broader continuum and can be part of a wider dialogue, but it must resist the temptation to be the end point of the dialogue. For Rupert Wegerif, monological thinking has its uses, as long as it resists that. He writes:

> Dialogues of the kind that lie behind progress in the natural sciences often include utterances of great length. Being able to work alone for long periods developing a coherent understanding of a domain of knowledge in the way that Einstein did, for example, is tremendously useful for the quality of the larger dialogue. But it is useful not for finally finding an ultimate theory of everything that all others will have to accept. It is useful for fashioning more insightful and valuable contributions to the ongoing dialogue of humanity (what Oakeshott referred to as the conversation of mankind). (Wegerif, 2013: 30)

In this sense, a monologic dynamic, where either the teacher is didactically speaking to students or where the student themselves is engaged in solitary thought, is a key element in the spirit of dialogism, but with one important caveat: it must then be appropriated into a dialogic mode of knowledge construction through inauthenticity, a term I shall return to later. This is an illuminating idea in an age where too much teacher talk is seen as bad practice, although it is interesting to note that in 2014 Ofsted offered guidance noting that inspectors should not criticize teacher talk for being overlong or bemoan a lack of opportunity for different activities in lessons. Wegerif goes on to note that:

> Monological thinking is good for dialogue as long as it does not become conceited and think that it is everything, at which point it becomes the voice of authority and closes down the dialogue. Einstein presented his theories as arising out of a creative dialogue with nature as a whole. There was no incompatibility between his dialogic orientation towards the cosmos and also towards his colleagues and the extraordinarily systematic and rigorous quality of his theories. (Wegerif, 2013: 30)

However, for Bakhtin the fundamental problematic aspect of monological thinking and discourse is that it is cut off from the very entities that can infuse it with meaning – namely, other voices. Meaning is located in the particular and not the collective, and thus enacts a reduced, myopic and 'particular' understanding of what is being discussed.

It should be stressed, however, that what Bakhtin means by a multitude of voices is not in fact a kind of aggregation of various kinds of thought into a unified, but ultimately compromised, whole, but rather a synthesis of voices into what can best be described as a harmonious unity. A useful way of thinking about this is to use the analogy of music, as Alexander Sidorkin illustrates:

> Truth for Bakhtin requires a multitude of bearers. Truth fundamentally cannot be contained within a single consciousness. It simply cannot be expressed with 'a single mouth': it needs many voices. Now, Bakhtin does not mean to say that many voices carry partial truth, each in its own way. For instance, if one hears two different opinions on the same subject, the truth is not deducible by 'averaging' the two, or by 'synthesizing' the opinions. A statement like 'the truth is somewhere in the middle' is not at all what Bakhtin had in mind. He apparently had a very different conception of truth. Truth is revealed when one can hear and comprehend both voices simultaneously, and more than that, when his or her own voice joins in and creates something similar to a musical chord. (Sidorkin, 1996: 20)

This rather poetic description is something which many teachers may view as a romantic idealization, where the job of teaching is often seen as knowledge dissemination and a periodic summative assessment of that process. The disrupting element in that process is the advent and ubiquity of technology, and specifically the ease of access to large bodies of data and information. How pupils manipulate that data and use it for knowledge construction is in many respects the elephant in the room that schools, policy-makers and governing bodies are struggling to address.

To return to the trivium for a moment, the Socratic method of *elenchus* is one way of approaching dialogue in the classroom to engender a landscape where there are no sacred cows, where every opinion can be interrogated without restraint and where all opinions are countered with their diametric other. As Martin Robinson explains:

> Socratic method is a form of argument called *elenchus* – refutation and cross examination; it is great fun for those involved if all are happy to participate, it is however quite threatening to those who are not, they can see it as upsetting and quite aggressive. What the questioner tries to do is look for contradictions and inconsistencies in answers and by the time the session is finished most often participants find themselves in a state of *Aporia* or doubt about quite fundamental things. This is the heart of the Socratic dialectical form of questioning, with many people often ending up none the wiser. (Robinson, 2014b)

So what does a truly dialogic interaction look like in the classroom? Well, to start off with, the relational interplay between pupil and teacher in a dialogic classroom assumes a fluid dynamic. For example, instead of having the teacher ask questions which are then answered 'correctly' by a pupil, what might occur is an ongoing dialogue where the pupil and teacher ask questions not of each other, but of the text itself and possible interpretations of it. An illustration of a 'finalized' exchange might look like this:

Example 1

Teacher: 'What does the red in this poem symbolize?'

Pupil: 'Blood.'

Teacher: 'Correct.'

Here, not only are the teacher and pupil roles fixed, but the relation to subject and meaning is at once static and final. There is no transition or communal interaction from their monologic positions. For Bakhtin, true dialogic expression is 'unfinalizable'; it is eternally unfinished and always orientated towards a future responder. That is to say, a final meaning cannot be truly arrived at in this closed way. In direct contrast to the last example, a dialogic exchange might look like this:

Example 2

Teacher: 'What could the red in this poem mean?'

Pupil: 'Could it symbolize blood?'

Teacher: 'Whose blood?'

Pupil: 'Could it be the blood of the [central character]?'

Teacher: 'Possibly, or could it be a political statement?'

Pupil: 'Was the author politically motivated?'

Teacher: 'Well, can you find any evidence from the text that might support that view?'

In this example, although the teacher is facilitating the discussion, there are no clearly defined roles: both teacher and pupil are creating meaning by asking questions of each other, and never quite arriving at a fixed meaning. It is also evident that, in this exchange, a far higher level of engagement with the text is present, where a more sophisticated exploration takes place rather than a simple 'X = Y' conclusion.

'Inauthenticity' and Bakhtin's Internally Persuasive Discourse

One constant refrain today in many spheres of education seems to be the injunction to be authentic, to 'be yourself' – and that by looking inward and uncovering the 'real you', an individual can achieve anything. It is as if there is one definitive version of yourself that you should always defer to, and if you don't do this, you are somehow being less than honest. This is a damaging development in education, I believe, and it has its roots in the self-help industry, which asserts a deficit model of humanity to further claims that are often unhelpful to the broader enterprise of education. It is also symptomatic of an increasingly narcissistic culture that is increasingly focused on the individual, and which wrongly claims that there is a singular 'truth' about yourself that can be discovered through esoteric 'new age' practices such as mindfulness or meditation.

The reality is that we are a mess of contradictions and inconsistencies, many of which we are completely unaware of. Instead of looking inward to find our 'true voice', Bakhtin claims we should be doing the opposite. We should be looking outward, adopting the voices of others and appropriating the best elements of those we admire in order to move away from our own biases and entrenched positions. We should be 'inauthentic' – but this is something that is very much out of vogue today. In fact, it is socially unacceptable in many quarters. Andrew Keen writes:

> I pride myself on my own inauthenticity. All my role models – Machiavelli, Hitchcock, Dylan, Bunuel – are artists of the inauthentic, of inventing one's inner life, of not being quite who we appear to be. (Keen, 2008)

Instead of getting students to ruminate on facile motivational posters or adopt the lotus position in search of their inner child, we should encourage them to read more, to consume as much knowledge as they can, to question their own certainties, biases and suppositions, and ultimately to celebrate their inconsistencies, not deny them.

One way to begin doing this is to adopt the voice of the other. In typically poetic style, Bakhtin outlines what he considers to be the internalization of meaning as 'internally persuasive discourse' (IPD). This refers to a process where the individual becomes involved in a form of co-ownership with the speaker. He writes:

> Internally persuasive discourse – as opposed to one that is externally authoritative – is, as it is affirmed through assimilation, tightly interwoven with 'one's own word'. In the everyday rounds of our consciousness, the internally persuasive word is half-ours and half-someone else's. (Bakhtin, 1981: 346)

There are clearly emancipatory possibilities for an IPD approach – but not always. Wertsch (2002) makes a distinction between two types of internalization: mastery and appropriation. He explores how students can 'master' a subject such as historical narrative without actually believing any of it thus not experiencing internal persuasion. This is in direct opposition to a dynamic where an individual will arrive at a place of internalization of their own volition, which has not been imposed through authority.

A set of simple cues given to students before discussion can help this, and can stop students from adopting and retaining fixed positions. For example, instruct students to use the following topic starters when they enter the dialogue:

> Following on from X's point ...
>
> To build on what X said ...
>
> Another point to consider in relation to what X said is ...
>
> I can see why X would say ______. However, ...
>
> If we take X's point at face value, then we have to accept that ...

Matusov and von Duyke (2010) develop this idea, referring to a second interpretation of IPD within a communal sense that focuses on student authorship. This method stresses the importance of the student becoming a valid member of 'a community of practice' in which not only do they internalize other positions but they also begin to author a truth for themselves through the process of writing. Matusov and von Duyke write:

> This means that we are aware that our words cannot be understood without the consideration of the words of others – the meaning of our words emerge and exist on the border of our and others' voices. In IPD, words are 'half-ours and half-someone else's' not in the past, but in the present because they are defined by, at least, by two distinct voices: our own and someone else's. (Matusov and von Duyke, 2010: 178)

Many educationalists today emphasize the importance of creativity. Yet to be creative, we are told, one has to find one's 'element' or true self. Again, I reiterate the claim that the first step in finding this 'true self' is the acceptance that there isn't one, and that the way to be truly creative is to become disinterred from the notion that there is one version of yourself, and to sing Whitman and Greenspan's refrain that in fact, you 'contain multitudes' (2005).

The nature of the contemporary classroom means that there are often nascent ideas from both student and teacher that are nebulous and open to critique. These ideas are often highly creative in nature and can be the pivotal point in a lesson, opening a door to new thought and enquiry. The spirit of IPD stresses the primacy of this state, that is without authoritative discourse yet aware of others' voices. As previously stated, Bakhtin (1981: 345) writes about the word that is only partly ours:

> Its creativity and productiveness consist precisely in the fact that such a word awakens new and independent words, that it organizes masses of our words from within, and does not remain in an isolated and static condition ... it enters into inter-animating relationships with new contexts. More than that, it enters into an intense interaction, a struggle with other internally persuasive discourses.

This 'intense interaction' is a feature of the best classroom discussions, and occurs both internally and externally. It is characterized by a rejection of certainty and an almost dangerously subversive, yet creative, process that is as unpredictable as it is tangible and that recalls Keats' notion of negative capability. Pollard (2008: 3) notes:

> One way of understanding internally persuasive discourse is the capacity to hold two or more contradictory 'positions' (beliefs, opinions or perspectives) simultaneously: however, unlike dialectical reasoning, it does not supersede these contradictions with a synthesis of ideas, but continues to throw up new contradictions. Internally persuasive discourse is one of Bakhtin's least referred to, but most important, concepts, although it can be challenging and disturbing to cherished beliefs. It is the antithesis of dogma and received wisdom.

Once again here is the seemingly cognitively dissonant notion that the trivium offers: of holding two irreconcilable ideas at once as a means of illuminating meaning. By adopting the voice of the other, we often find our own 'inauthentic' voice.

Carnival and the Public Square

In ancient Greece, the Agora (meaning 'open place of assembly') was a public space where people came to hold a free exchange of ideas and openly debate contested topics. The original Agora of Athens was where Socrates would openly question market stallholders – and anyone else for that matter – on their presuppositions and biases around a particular philosophical issue. It was here that a young Plato listened to Socrates and then went home and burned all his books as a result of the transformational ideas he had heard.

This idea of a particular time and space occupying the potential for powerful dialogue is at the heart of Bakhtin's philosophy, and one he incorporates into his notion of the public square, which he describes as the 'symbol of communal performance' (Bakhtin, 1984: 128). He also marries this with the idea of carnival. He writes:

> Carnival is a pageant without footlights and without a division into performers and spectators. In carnival everyone is an active participant; everyone communes in the carnival act. Carnival is not contemplated, and, strictly speaking, not even performed; its participants live in it, they live by its laws as long as those laws are in effect; that is, they live a carnivalesque life. Because carnivalistic life is life drawn out of its usual rut, it is to some extent 'life turned inside out'. (Bakhtin, 1984: 122)

The central idea of Bakhtin's 'carnival' is one of playful subversion or a sort of positive anarchy, where traditional roles are subverted and alternative ones assumed. In medieval times, the carnival manifested itself in the form of masked balls and ritual celebrations, and represented a way of society renewing itself in particular ways. Of course, this idea is confined to a particular time and space, and if it were to become the norm then it would lose its inherent power. Along with the idea of a public space, these ideas represent an opportunity for individuals to step outside themselves, assume a different viewpoint, and contemplate competing claims from a very different perspective.

However, these ideas are under attack in education today, particularly in universities, where many are calling for a 'safe space' from challenging views, where certain perspectives are censored and even banned, and for 'trigger warnings' on certain works of literature, in case they offend. Indeed, at Columbia University in New York, a small group of students succeeded in having Ovid taken off a particular syllabus because of the potentially triggering content of his work (Gitlin, 2015). Bakhtin would have strongly objected to such a closing down of dialogue and the limiting of meaning. He was a great advocate of humour as a means of creating meaning, and shifting people from entrenched positions – and the more offensive, the better!

A central problem with much of what pupils write today is that it's written for an audience of one. Students write work that is then assessed by the teacher in a loop. One way of confronting this is by creating spaces where students can work within the 'public square' and engage with competing voices and positions. By giving students an arena where it is not simply their teacher reading their work but their peers, parents and the wider online community, they learn very rapidly to craft their work more carefully and be more attentive to its final result. This is perhaps best illustrated in the way students interact online today, where every post and comment is recorded. Neil Mercer et al. (2007: 3) write that: 'In the 1990s, classroom-based observational research by ourselves and other colleagues, revealed that much of the interaction taking place was not of any obvious educational value.'

In too many situations, students see group work as an opportunity to chat about other issues, or to let stronger students lead, or even to contribute nothing at all. The problem here is one of accountability. Mercer et al. (2007: 4) continue (in reference to exploratory talk): 'Students should be encouraged in such discussions to make all relevant knowledge *publicly accountable*.'

This notion of 'all relevant knowledge' being 'publicly accountable' is given a new and perhaps radical possibility through the technological affordances of online collaboration. A document that is editable online can be shared with an entire class during or outside a lesson, and pupils are directly accountable for what they write.

Equally significant is what pupils *don't* write in a virtual space. When pupils are given a task in which they are asked to write down an introductory sentence or paragraph to a proposed essay, what is often observed is a completely different dynamic to classroom discussion. The more orally confident pupils will often write nothing until other pupils have written something down. They will wait, staring at their screens, and when five or so examples have been written, only then will they write something. The fact that their work is 'publicly accountable' transforms the task and its learning possibilities – it changes what they write and how they think, and questions fixed biases and positions.

As teachers we should re-create the idea of the public square to facilitate a free and open exchange of ideas, in which students are open to shifting their own positions and presuppositions in the spirit of the carnival. We should not, of course, allow students to be openly cruel or create an intimidating atmosphere, but instead we should encourage a serious, yet playful, space that enacts Bakhtin's idea of 'life turned inside out' (Bakhtin, 1984: 122).

The 'Speech Genre' of Academic Writing

In terms of writing in a particular voice (i.e. the privileged academic voice of the more able student), Bakhtin's concept of speech genres has much to say – about writing in an arena that is increasingly characterized by technology and where there is a plethora of voices and genres of writing instantly available. Bakhtin defines speech genres thus: 'Each separate utterance is individual, of course, but each sphere in which language is used develops its own relatively stable types of these utterances. These we may call speech genres' (Bakhtin, 1986: 60).

When we think of student academic writing, and particularly the often very precise 'speech genre' required of A level English, for example, it is clear that there is a specific lexical field that the student must enter in order to be recognized as a higher-level student in terms of summative assessment. Within different speech genres, there are a discrete set of rules that produce a particular effect. Interestingly, Bakhtin does not privilege this academic speech genre against a perhaps less refined social discourse. He writes:

> Many people who have an excellent command of a language often feel quite helpless in certain spheres of communication precisely because they do not have a practical command of the generic forms used in given spheres. Frequently a person who has an excellent command of speech in some areas of cultural communication, who is able to read a scholarly paper or engage in a scholarly discussion, who speaks very well on social questions, is silent or very awkward in social conversation. Here it is not a matter of an impoverished vocabulary or of style, taken abstractly: this is entirely a matter of the inability to command a repertoire of genres of social conversation. (1986: 78)

Bakhtin's rejection of the traditional perspective of an 'impoverished vocabulary' speaks to his championing of the disenfranchised, and offers perhaps a new perspective on the types of new speech genres and idiolects that are created through online interaction.

Again, for Bakhtin the reductive force of the monologic, authoritative voice is one that ultimately limits meaning. This can be juxtaposed with the IPD of dialogic enquiry, in which the individual probes, questions and reorientates meaning. For Theresa Lillis, the latter position offers the most fertile ground for student academic writing:

> This second level radically challenges not only the more obvious monologue practices surrounding student academic writing (for example, the standard practice of the tutor setting an essay question to which the student responds in accordance with the knowledge that has been authorised in lectures, seminars and course materials) but also a key dimension of the epistemology upon which the Western academy is founded; that is, on a particular version of dialectic, a 'monologic-dialectic' from a Bakhtinian perspective. (Lillis, 2003: 204)

A Bakhtinian approach to academic writing also invites us to view a student's work in a process of becoming; that is, not being in a fixed, finalized state. Lillis continues:

> One relatively simple way of involving students in decisions about the kinds of meanings they might wish to make in their academic writing, and thus a shift towards a more dialogic approach, is to reconceptualise the widespread practice of 'feedback' as 'talkback'. (Lillis, 2003: 204)

For Bakhtin, this interchangeability of interlocution is central to the creation of meaning: 'Any understanding is imbued with response and necessarily elicits it in one form or another: the listener becomes the speaker' (Bakhtin, 1986: 68–69). This radical proposal of subverting roles speaks to another Bakhtinian concept: the carnivalesque – a dynamic of structured chaos to elicit creativity. Again, this is an entirely apposite prism through which to view the use of classroom dialogue in education today.

Conclusion

One of the most powerful aspects of the trivium is that, by its very structure, it challenges dogmatic modes of thinking and entrenched positions. Through its three constituent parts, we are encouraged to fuse meaning through multiple perspectives and positions. In many ways it is an act of bravery to do so in an age where everyone appears to be so certain about everything and has the power of the internet to prove it.

We want our students to leave a classroom having been really stretched and challenged, to have them thinking about a particular lesson or topic for hours afterwards, and to create the potential for them to adopt the voice of the other in order to better understand competing perspectives. Bakhtin knew that this could not be achieved by closing off discussion and dialogue and limiting the search for truth. Instead he proposed accepting our contradictions, inconsistencies and imperfections and bringing them to the dialogue in a process of opening up meaning.

> Truth is not born, nor is it to be found inside the head of an individual person, it is born between people collectively searching for truth, in the process of their dialogic interaction. (Bakhtin, 1984: 110)

References

Bakhtin, Mikhail M. (1981) *The Dialogic Imagination: Four Essays*. Michael Holquist (ed.), Caryl Emerson and Michael Holquist (tr.). Austin and London: University of Texas Press.

Bakhtin, Mikhail M. (1984) *Problems of Dostoevsky's Poetics*, Caryl Emerson (ed. and tr.). Manchester: Manchester University Press.

Bakhtin, Mikhail M. and Emerson, Caryl (1986) *Speech Genres and Other Late Essays*, Michael Holquist (ed.), Vern W. McGee (tr.). Austin, TX: University of Texas Press.

Gitlin, Todd (2015) 'Why are Student Protesters so Fearful?', *New York Times* Opinion. Available at: www.nytimes.com/2015/11/22/opinion/sunday/why-are-student-protesters-so-fearful.html.

Keen, Andrew (2008) 'On (in)authenticity', *Andrew Keen* [blog] (31 July). Available at: www.ajkeen.com/blog/2008/07/31/on-inauthentici.

Lillis, Theresa (2003) 'Student Writing as "Academic Literacies": Drawing on Bakhtin to Move from Critique to Design', *Language and Education*, 17(3): 192–207.

Matusov, Eugene (2004) 'Bakhtin's Debit in Educational Research: Dialogic Pedagogy', *Journal of Russian and East European Psychology*, 42(6): 3–11.

Matusov, Eugene and von Duyke, Katherine (2010) 'Bakhtin's Notion of the *Internally* Persuasive Discourse in Education: Internal to what? (A case of discussion of issues of foul language in teacher education)'. In Karin Junefelt and Pia Nordin (eds), *Proceedings from the Second International Interdisciplinary Conference on Perspectives and Limits of Dialogism in Mikhail Bakhtin: Stockholm University, Sweden June 3–5, 2009*: 174–199.

Mercer, Neil, Dawes, Lyn, Sams, Claire, et al. (2007) 'Computers, Literacy and Thinking Together'. In Anthony Adams and Sue Brindley (eds), *Teaching Secondary English with ICT*. Maidenhead: Open University Press, pp. 1–17.

Pollard, Rachel (2008) *Dialogue and Desire: Mikhail Bakhtin and the Linguistic Turn in Psychotherapy*. London: Karnac.

Putnam, Hilary (1992) 'Is There a Fact of the Matter about Fiction?'. In James Conant (ed.), *Realism with a Human Face*. Cambridge, MA: Harvard University Press, pp. 209–213.

Robinson, Martin (2013) *Trivium 21c: Preparing Young People for the Future with Lessons from the Past*. Carmarthen: Independent Thinking Press.

Robinson, Martin (2014a) 'On Dialectic: Dissoi Logoi – Teaching the Trivium', *Trivium21c* [blog] (22 December). Available at: https://martinrobborobinson.wordpress.com/2014/12/22/on-dialectic-dissoi-logoi-teaching-the-trivium/.

Robinson, Martin (2014b) 'The Socratic Method, Teaching the Trivium: Dialectic', *Trivium21c* [blog] (29 December). Available at: https://martinrobborobinson.wordpress.com/2014/12/29/the-socratic-method-teaching-the-trivium-dialectic/.

Sidorkin, Alexander (1996) 'An Ontological Understanding of Dialogue in Education.' PhD thesis, University of Washington.

Wegerif, Rupert (2013) *Dialogic: Education for the Internet Age*. London: Routledge.

Wertsch, James (2002) *Voices of Collective Remembering*. Cambridge: Cambridge University Press.

Whitman, Walt and Greenspan, Ezra (2005) *Walt Whitman's 'Song of Myself': A Sourcebook and Critical Edition*. New York: Routledge.

Chapter 9

Philosophically Powerful Projects

Dr John L. Taylor

In this chapter, Dr John Taylor (Director of the Philosophy in Education project, and Director of Learning, Teaching and Innovation at the Cranleigh School in Surrey), describes a model for philosophically rich project work. Taylor, who has many years of experience in both the teaching of philosophy and the development of project work, makes the case that a combination of philosophical discussion and project work provides an ideal context for implementing a number of the elements in the trivium curriculum model. Philosophical enquiry, through discussion, proceeds most fruitfully when it is structured using the principles of grammar, dialectic and rhetoric: that is to say, when the conversation takes the form of an informed, structured, reasoned debate, in which students are explicitly taught techniques of argumentation and given support in the challenging task of making oral presentations of their opinions to others. Discursive learning of this sort is naturally complemented by project work – a process of sustained, critical, reflective enquiry. This provides the context within which ideas can germinate, and the embryonic capacities of 'philosopher kids' can further be nurtured and strengthened.

The Lost Love of Learning

Recent years have been dominated by a programme of qualification reform. Underpinning some of the changes is research that expresses concerns about sixth-form teaching and learning from those in higher education whose role it is to assess our students, the products of our sixth forms. A study of the attitudes of higher education (HE) admissions officers towards A levels, commissioned by Ofqual and carried out by IPSOS MORI in 2012, found that while there is broad satisfaction with the content of A level qualifications, there is disquiet about the way that sixth-form students learn (Higton et al., 2012). Interviewees noted that the ability of students to think critically about what they are learning is not being developed. They tend to accept uncritically the information supplied to them by their teachers. There is also a failure to develop a synoptic understanding of a subject – with, for example, a lack of awareness of meta-narrative in history.

Underpinning these perceived problems, interviewees felt, is a philosophically deficient approach to learning. A level students tend to lack intellectual curiosity. Interviewees commented that they lack a love of learning. A culture of spoon-feeding and 'teaching to the test' has taken the place of learning for its own sake. Learning has come to be valued for utilitarian reasons:

> Many were of the opinion that the number of exams taken within A levels meant that pupils had no opportunity to gain a love of their subject and had encouraged a '*joyless little bean-counter*' approach to learning, whereby they thought that learning was simply a matter of knowing the right answer. However, it was noted by this interviewee and others that this utilitarian approach to learning and exam-passing is something that is embedded in the entire education

> system, and not solely an issue in the A level system. (Higton et al., 2012: 79)

We have witnessed the reduction of learning to a process of training students to jump through assessment hoops. This reduction of education has occurred on account of a 'utilitarian' approach which sees the value of what is learned solely in terms of measurable outcomes.

This accurate, if pessimistic, diagnosis does, however, suggest a possible solution. The problem can be traced back to its roots in a philosophical theory of what makes learning valuable; the unmistakable inference is that the problem we face is, in part, a philosophical one. If that is so, perhaps the way ahead lies in the creation of a new philosophical approach to learning.

It is very much in the spirit of the trivium to suppose that philosophy could provide a remedy for at least some of education's ills. An obvious way to concoct a cure would be through philosophical reflection on the nature of learning, teaching and assessment, and the creation of qualifications that are designed to replace 'teaching to the test' with something philosophically more inspiring – namely, a process of teaching students to think for themselves. As we will see, the Extended Project Qualification (EPQ) is just such a philosophical remedy.

A Brief History of the Extended Project Qualification

The roots of the EPQ can be traced back to the development of an AS level project-based programme in the history, philosophy and ethics of science, called Perspectives on Science, which was piloted between 2004 and 2008. This course was designed to enable students to develop their own ideas about philosophical and ethical questions arising from science. The programme of study was designed to give students the tools and the opportunity to begin thinking for themselves. With that aim in mind, the decision to reject a terminal examination and opt instead for assessment through project work made perfect sense.

The Perspectives course served as a prototype for the EPQ, which was launched in 2008. The EPQ is an A level standard qualification. It is assessed by means of a research project and an oral presentation. EPQ students choose to write a dissertation, produce a performance, create an artefact or carry out a scientific investigation or field study. Project work takes around 80 hours and can occupy anything from a single term up to the full two years of the sixth form.

The EPQ was created to provide a higher educational model of learning in a secondary context. Those of us who worked on its development were conscious of the need to help smooth out the transition between secondary and higher education and, as things have turned out, the EPQ has been welcomed by academics precisely because of its value as a preparation for university study. It was seen by interviewees in the IPSOS MORI survey to address many of the weaknesses identified within A levels, providing a context for students to think more deeply and independently, and to pursue connections between different elements of the subjects they are learning:

> We're very keen on the Extended Project [Qualification], and very, very positive about it. We make alternate offers sometimes – we might make, say, an A*AA offer excluding the Extended Project, and then an A*AB offer including the Extended Project, and give somebody an either/or. The Extended Project [provides the] thinking skills that we're interested in. (Admissions Staff, HEI, England quoted in Higton et al., 2012: 73)

The sentiment is shared widely. In 2012, speaking at the London Institute of Economics, Schools Minister Elizabeth Truss remarked that the EPQ 'develops and rewards creative and independent thought as well as research and planning. It represents the best of education, in that it is rigorous and demanding as well as adaptable and fun' (Truss, 2012).

Teachers are keen too. One teacher on the Perspectives on Science course said:

> I am really enthusiastic about the course. I think it's probably the most enjoyable teaching I've ever done in my whole teaching career. I think it's because for once the students and I are actually exploring knowledge, for the love of exploring knowledge, rather than trying to prove that Ohm's Law is still Ohm's Law. (Levinson et al., 2008: 29)

Given the alignment between the EPQ and the type of independent learning valued by universities, it is not surprising to find that there is a growing body of evidence indicating that taking an EPQ improves a student's chances of getting a university place. For example, a recent study found that:

> Regarding some of the recently introduced academic qualifications, this research showed that having an Extended Project Qualification or a Cambridge Pre-U GPR qualification alongside AS/A levels significantly increased the probability of attending a university in the Russell or 1994 groups. These qualifications, which require research and autonomous working, have been praised by universities, especially competitive ones, as they allow the development of independent research skills needed for undergraduate study. It is therefore not surprising that they provide 'better' access to competitive universities. (Rodeiro et al., 2015: 19)

In the EPQ, then, we have an antidote to the spoon-feeding and 'teaching to the test' culture, one which successfully prepares sixth-form students for the challenge of higher education, where they will be expected to work with greater independence and show personal commitment to their chosen subject of study.

Most EPQ programmes involve a taught element, in which students are taught the skills they will need for their projects and are given an opportunity to explore a range of ideas, so that when they come to choose the title for their project, they make an informed choice, and enter the project work phase equipped with the tools they need to do the job. In what follows, we will first explore the nature of the pedagogy that informs the taught-course basis of an EPQ programme, then move on to examine the project work phase.

The Trivium 21c curriculum model is structured around the principles of grammar (foundational knowledge), dialectic (argumentative engagement) and rhetoric (the expression of ideas). As we will see, grammar, dialectic and rhetoric feature within the taught element of philosophically rich EPQ programmes, and these self-same principles serve to provide structure and direction to the process of project work as well.

I argue, then, that the rich educational experience of many EPQ students derives from the application of educational principles that are recognizably part of the Trivium 21c model. The pedagogy of the EPQ – an innovative modern qualification – has its roots in traditional philosophical thought.

Philosophy: The Grammar of Enquiry

There is no doubting the efficacy of philosophical questions as a stimulant of thought. In a physics class, the question 'What came before the Big Bang?' is liable to ignite lively debate about the possibility of a first cause. In an English lesson, a study of *Hamlet* might well engender debate about personal identity. Likewise, a class studying French Literature might well, when reading Camus, find themselves discussing the meaning of life. The nature of art could be debated within an art lesson, and so on.

Classroom conversations like these, in my experience, have a catalytic effect – they energize lessons, turning otherwise passive students into vocal contributors to a lively debate. They are points at which education moves beyond being a passive process of absorption of facts into a shared journey of enquiry, in which the point is not to tell the students what to think, but for them to begin thinking for themselves.

Aside from their intrinsic interest and educational value, conversations like this are a rich and valuable starting point for research projects. If our aim, then, is to prepare students for work on a research project, there is considerable value in beginning with a series of seminars in which philosophical discussion is used as a catalyst for enquiry.

As well as their catalytic role, the opening lessons of a programme of project-based learning can serve a number of other purposes, including training in the skills needed for project work, exploration of possible topic areas, and some preliminary teaching of important theoretical frameworks. In the terms of *Trivium 21c*, such lessons involve teaching the 'grammar' that will be needed for project work. Grammar is an apt metaphor, insofar as it indicates the structural knowledge – the sets of frameworks – which need to be mastered before thoughts can be coherently formulated and ideas developed.

It is important to note that the knowledge base which is taught at the outset of an EPQ course is constrained by the fact that the purpose of the taught course is to prepare students to research and think for themselves. It is not necessary, nor appropriate, to teach everything that students might need to know about a given topic. On the contrary, the point of the taught course is to equip them to learn independently. The scaffolding must be put in place and the student handed the tools they need to begin building for themselves.

The material which is used as the basis for these discussions has, therefore, to be carefully selected for its utility in preparing students to learn independently. In practice, this means selecting case studies that fulfil a number of roles. First, the content of the case studies should be stimulating. It should provoke questioning and inspire curiosity, since part of the function of the taught course is to inspire students to enquire for themselves.

Second, the case studies should enable the teaching of specific skills, such as research or argument analysis. Third, they should provide the grammatical structure of specific debates: the framework of knowledge which is needed for meaningful enquiry to begin.

The phrase I have coined for the task of the teacher in such lessons is Socratic mentoring. Just as Socrates saw it as his life's work to challenge people to think for themselves about the concepts which they used, unreflectively, during their everyday life, and to become aware of the limits of their knowledge, so the Socratic mentor seeks to stimulate students to begin to think for themselves, and, on becoming aware that they lack answers, to begin to enquire.

To illustrate how this might work in the classroom, consider the topic of personal identity. What am I? Is there something within me which, despite all the changes I have undergone since my birth, remains constant? Can I be identified with the set of roles I play in life?

This is a topic which tends to prompt lively discussion and debate. One way of exploring it is via thought experiments: imaginary scenarios which invite us to explore our concept of personal identity by seeing how it would apply if, for example, we were to undergo sudden and total memory loss, or experience a brain transplant operation. Less bizarrely, asking students whether they think their clothes are part of their personal identity, or their social media activity, can lead to interesting discussion of whether identity and personality are the same.

This discussion can be taken further by introducing extracts from the writings of philosophers who have grappled with the problem, such as John Locke, who entertained a thought experiment in which the soul of a cobbler entered the body of a prince, and also introduced us to a putatively rational parrot – a bird which, the story had it, could converse in English (Locke, 1975 [1689]: 333). Would not such a bird count as a person? Locke thought that it would, and this showed that the concept of a person could be separated from that of a human being, personhood being determined by the possession of a mental life involving conscious thought (a faculty which could, in imagination at least, occur in non-human animals). Taking the discussion in this direction brings ethical concerns into focus: is our reluctance to ascribe personhood to non-human animals a sign of an inherent bias in favour of humanity?

Providing a little more of the grammar of the debate, three theories of personal identity can be introduced. One is the theory that being the same person is a matter of having the same body (physical continuity). Another is the theory that what matters is possession of the same mind (psychological continuity). A third is that what underpins personal identity is sameness of soul. Theories such as these provide a helpful framework for developing the discussion. Students could be asked to examine sources from the literature, such as extracts from the writing of John Locke, or more recent contributors such as Derek Parfit, and identify arguments for and against each theory. They could then engage in a class debate about the relative merits of these different accounts of personhood. In this way, grammar (learning some of the elements of the philosophical discussion of personal identity) serves to enable dialectic (argumentative engagement) and rhetoric (contributing to a class debate).

Philosophical enquiry constitutes a fertile ground within which the seeds of ideas for projects can begin to germinate. They suggest questions which capture the student's imagination and so serve to prompt further exploration within an EPQ. A student might be inspired to produce a film illustrating the effect of memory loss on the sense of self, or examining how a sense of strong personal identity can persist even through dramatic bodily change, such as damage to one's face. The concept of personal identity can be explored on stage (e.g. through a production of *Hamlet*) or as it features in novels (such as Kafka's *The Metamorphosis*). Artwork offers another medium for response (the emergence of the self-portrait as a form of painting). The links to ethics could be explored: should we count humans at the very beginning or end of life as persons? If a person has irretrievably lost the capacity for consciousness, are they still rightly called a person? Should we widen the sphere of personhood to include, say, the great apes?

Our example shows, then, the fertility of philosophical topics as starting points for a wide range of potential projects. Philosophical discussion about knowledge, truth, myth, reality, freedom, consciousness, value, beauty or justice also works well in this regard. Such conversations raise the 'big questions'. They expose the perennially problematic ideas that lie beneath the surface of more or less every topic that students might study. A philosophical question is an invitation to begin a journey of enquiry into the unknown.

All this said, it is true that some students sit through lessons like these wondering what the point is, since they have already made up their mind that their project will be about something totally different. But these philosophical explorations have surprisingly wide application. Suppose a student has decided to write a project about the pay of footballers in the Premiership. He (it usually is a he) might be surprised to find that some philosophy can help. For as soon as questions such as 'What is a fair wage?' or 'What is the point of sport?' are asked, we enter the domain of ethics. Some appreciation of the grammar of ethics, in the form of familiarization with widely held ethical theories, will be a useful part of the toolkit for many students, giving them some knowledge to draw on when seeking to organize their research and formulate lines of argument and counter-argument.

In the case of the Extended Project, students are expected to take a topic and probe more deeply, or widely, by making links between areas of learning. Philosophical enquiry involves just this sort of meta-cognitive, analytical thought. It is a form of enquiry which aims at achieving synopticity (that is, an overview of a conceptual terrain as a whole). Raising questions such as 'What is justice?' or 'Is there an objective standard for beauty or goodness?' can lead to deep, probing thought, ranging across all areas of the syllabus. Philosophical discussion is thus an effective antidote to the reduction of real education to a soulless regime of spoon-feeding of 'bite-sized' disjointed packets of information, and an excellent preparation for deep, rich project work.

Teaching Dialectic

If philosophical discussion can serve to initiate enquiry, the journey itself is powered by dialectic: a process of ongoing argument between contrary points of view. When we come to examine the nature of student activity during the development of their projects, we will see that the best projects are driven forward by a process of continual questioning, arguing and counter-arguing. The process approximates to the method of dialectic in which one point (a thesis) is countered by another (the antithesis), and the tension is resolved (through synthesis).

Argument and counter-argument are at the heart of this process. Therefore, in the opening phase of an EPQ course, students should be given opportunities to engage argumentatively as much as possible, and should also be taught some of the principles of dialectic.

In some courses, such as those on critical thinking, reasoning processes are taught in the abstract, via formal or semi-formal models of argument analysis. In the Extended Project, however, dialectic is best taught contextually. Students are taught to reason by means of drawing them into specific discussions of philosophical questions, from which general points about the structure of effective argument can then emerge. So, for example, there may be classroom debates about God and science, about the existence of free will or about the ethical treatment of animals. From these debates, points about the structure of dialectic may be drawn out.

Rather than discussing the logical structure of argument in great technical depth, I prefer to teach students a relatively simple dialectical model, explaining to them that they can use this structure when analysing source materials, engaging in further discussion or debate, or during the writing of their project. It looks like this:

Point of view:	The proposition being defended in the argument.

Argument:	The chain of reasons that support the point of view.
Counter-argument:	Criticism of the argument, showing that it does not succeed in supporting the point of view (the argument is invalid, and/or contains unwarranted assumptions).
Response:	Defence of the original argument, either by modifying it so that it avoids the force of the counter-argument, or by an attack on the counter-argument.

Suppose, for example, that students are introduced to a debate about the nature of the human mind. A question such as 'Will science fully explain the mind?' could be posed. The question can be explored first by examining different sources which provide contrasting answers to this question. While examining sources, students can use the dialectical model to assist in critical reading of source materials. Can they identify the main point that is being put forward, then identify the logical argument which is used in defence of this point?

It could be, for example, that they read an extract from a column in a journal such as *New Scientist*, which argues that the best prospect for understanding the nature of the mind is through a materialist theory which identifies the mind with the brain. The evidence in support of this would be evidence of the success of the methodology of reductionism in the past, as applied to phenomena such as heat, light, sound, the spread of disease, or the formation and development of living things. The argument analysis would look like this:

Point:	The human mind can be explained scientifically.

Argument: Many mysterious phenomena such as heat, sound, disease and even life itself have been explained scientifically. Therefore it is reasonable to believe that science will explain the mind.

Once this argument is clearly identified, students can be asked to engage in critical evaluation. They may read a source such as Thomas Nagel's classic paper 'What is it like to be a bat?' which argues that consciousness is an essential feature of the mind and it is not reducible to an objective, scientifically explicable phenomenon (Nagel, 1974). So now we have the other side of the debate:

Counter-argument: The mind cannot be explained scientifically. Consciousness is a subjective phenomenon, and subjective phenomena cannot be scientifically explained. People may experience the world in quite different ways. I don't know what the colour blue looks like to you, and neither of us has the remotest idea what it is like to be a bat.

Having identified arguments and counter-arguments, students may be invited to engage in debate themselves. This step – the step from observing the dialectical process in action to becoming an active participant – is an important one. It is not a step that students find easy; they may be unsure of their views, and lack the necessary confidence to engage in the cut and thrust of debate. It is, however, an essential step if students are to move from being observers of the conversation of ideas to being active participants. In terms of the Trivium 21c model, it is the step from dialectical analysis to rhetorical engagement.

Teaching Rhetoric

'Rhetoric', Martin Robinson writes, with more than a nod to Matthew Arnold, 'is the expression of our learning, enabling us to take part in, and be a part of, the great conversation. … Rhetoric is where we strive to take part in the best that has been thought, said, and done' (Robinson, 2013: 232). As we have seen, it is within the context of philosophical conversation that the development of the knowledge and dialectical skills that project work requires can take place. Not least, conversation is appropriate since the philosophical nature of the topics being explored implies a lack of final certainties; there is little scope here for pronouncements from the teacher to act as the final word concerning the best of what has been thought, said or done. When we reach the edges of knowledge and encounter ambiguity, disagreement and uncertainty, the appropriate mode of engagement is dialogical. As David Hume noted in his elegant *Dialogues Concerning Natural Religion:*

> Any question of philosophy, on the other hand, which is so *obscure* and *uncertain*, that human reason can reach no fixed determination with regard to it; if it should be treated at all; seems to lead us naturally into the style of dialogue and conversation. Reasonable men may be allowed to differ, where no one can reasonably be positive. (Hume, 1990 [1779]: 38)

The seminar discussions that precede Extended Project work in many schools provide a rich and rewarding context for just such dialogue to take place. In the best discussions, the stimulus provided by differences of viewpoint leads to reasoned analysis of the arguments on either side of the debate.

Achieving this type of dialogical engagement between students calls for careful stage-setting on the part of the Socratic mentor. The development of rhetorical skill (the ability to participate in a reasoned discussion of significant ideas, rather than simple fluency) is something that can be achieved by a series of discursive activities, which pose progressively greater challenges to students. So, for example, a natural starting point would be a 'low risk' conversation, in which students are invited to interview a classmate then present their ideas to the rest of the group. A next step would be to explore a controversial topic with the expectation that they present their own opinions. Finally, they may be asked to engage in a class debate, a task which calls both for expression of views and for engagement in processes of argument and counter-argument.

Students and staff respond warmly to the opportunity to learn through conversation. In a research study of the Perspectives on Science course, students reported that they enjoyed the opportunity to learn in this way, and that these conversations often led them to challenge their own assumptions and, on occasion, to change their mind (Levinson et al., 2008: 9). The significance of having a juxtaposition of opposing viewpoints will come as no surprise to those who understand the necessity of a dialectical element in learning; the presence of divergent views is the catalyst for enquiry as to where truth lies. Indeed, we may go further and identify the presence of strongly opposing viewpoints as one of the hallmarks of successful classroom discussion.

The mention of divergent views, however, raises the concern that opening up space within the curriculum for free exchange of ideas may create conditions which could be used to steer young minds in dangerous directions. The use of the term 'rhetoric' in this context might appear unhelpful, since in modern parlance it is taken to mean speech that appeals solely to the emotions, bypassing reason. One contributor to an intriguing research paper on teaching approaches that can help young people develop resilience to extremism contrasted the benefits of dialogical teaching of skills in critical thinking with the dangers of rhetoric:

> These [critical thinking skills] are core skills that are going to benefit children and young people generally. But they are also going to benefit them in relation to not being sucked into extremist ideologies because they're going to be able to see through ... the rhetoric. (Project Leader, *Philosophy for Children,* cited in Bonnell et al., 2010: 78)

Is rhetoric, then, part of the problem? Is classroom discussion which involves discussion of strongly held, potentially extreme, views a liability? I suggest not. We need not dispense with rhetoric, but rather need to understand it correctly. In its beneficent form, rhetoric is neither more nor less than effective speech. According to Aristotle, it involves the use of logos (reason), ethos (style) and pathos (emotion). Provided we remain within the framework of rational debate, there may be passionately expressed views.

The danger arises from speech in which passion is used to sway the audience and reason is disregarded. But provided that the passionate presentation of ideas does not overwhelm or displace the use of reason, there is no call for pathos to be dispensed with. The form of speech which is encouraged in the Perspectives course is one that allies passion to reason, allowing scope for strongly held views to be presented, but with the expectation that they will be subject to rigorous logical analysis, and accepted, or rejected, not on the basis of the persuasive character of the speaker, but on the strength of the evidence adduced in their favour. As Levinson et al. note, strongly held (even extreme) views are not a block to effective classroom conversation, but a precondition of it:

> Diversity, passionate advocacy and positioning of extreme points of view are characteristics of good discussion. While passion and extreme points of view can sometimes appear intimidating to other students, teachers ought not to be unduly worried; indeed, such characteristics can be harnessed for productive discussion. (Levinson et al., 2008: 30)

The Grammar of Project Work

We have looked at how the taught component of an EPQ programme can be structured around the Trivium 21c principles of grammar, dialectic and rhetoric. We turn now to an examination of the process of project work, where we will find these principles continue to provide a helpful framework.

Grammar comes first: that is to say, there is little point in engaging in dialectical analysis of arguments, or rhetorical expression of points of view, unless the student first knows something about their topic. An EPQ is a research project, and research involves finding out what the student needs to know in order to make a meaningful, credible attempt to address a particular research question, or respond in a creatively viable fashion to a design brief.

It is for this reason that the majority of EPQ students are advised to begin their projects by writing a literature review. This is the stage in the process where students acquaint themselves with the ideas, theories and history behind their question. Writing a literature review is a matter of evidence gathering: it is, in terms of the trivium, a matter of acquiring the grammatical knowledge needed to contribute meaningfully to the discussion of the chosen research topic.

I tend to insist on a clear distinction, within written dissertations, between the literature review and the discussion section. In terms of the Trivium 21c model, this corresponds to the distinction between grammar and dialectic. We want students to engage in the process of argument and counter-argument, but we want them to do so on an informed basis. Hence the literature review (the summary of research) precedes the discussion (the statement of arguments).

A useful analogy is provided by a legal trial. The first stage in a trial is the evidence-gathering stage, when lawyers cross-examine witnesses or introduce objects to the court to provide the evidence on which they will subsequently go on to seek to prove the guilt or innocence of the defendant. In terms of a dissertation, writing the literature review corresponds to the evidence-gathering phase of a trial, and the discussion corresponds to the part of a trial when lawyers seek to use the evidence to make a case for the prosecution or defence. There is, then, a different style of writing that is appropriate to each section: the literature review should be written in an objective style, without the student declaring their hand. By contrast, the discussion section requires them to take sides and press the case for one particular answer to their research question.

The legal model can also help students to appreciate the connection between the literature review and the discussion. It is not uncommon for students to write their reviews of literature, examining what the sources have to say about their chosen topic, then put this to one side and write a more or less disconnected essay in which they express their own views but fail to provide much documentary evidence to support it. In the better projects, however, students appreciate the importance of basing their arguments on evidence, and understand how to make use of the sources they have investigated, either to provide material to support the cases they are making, or to give them points of view to argue against. In terms of the trivium, then, we have here another application of the principle that the ability to argue effectively depends upon the possession of relevant knowledge: dialectic builds on and makes use of grammar.

In practical projects, the focus is typically provided by a design brief or commission: a real or hypothetical client needs an object made or an event to take place. This might be a performance of a play for a specific audience (an adaptation of *Hamlet* for Year 9 students, for instance) or the creation of an artefact for a specific purpose (the design of a new carbon-neutral office block, for example, or an illustrated guidebook for a wildlife sanctuary).

During the planning phase of the project, the student works to produce a specification of how they intend to respond to the design brief or commission. Then follows a period of research into genre, stylistic influences and relevant materials, processes and techniques – this research is typically presented visually, in sketchbooks with annotated records of sources, photographs, artwork and design development sheets. A short literature review may also figure.

Dialectical Project Development

Once the student is well informed about the relevant facts and theories, they are expected to engage in writing the discussion or development section of their project. This is the heart of the project, where they put forward and defend their own point of view in answer to their chosen question. This section is explicitly dialectical. Students are expected to engage in a process of argument, with consideration of and response to counter-argument.

One of the aims of exploring philosophical topics with students, at the outset of the course, is to familiarize them with the process of engaging with a range of opinions. If the first step in the process is to teach the importance of supporting ideas with reasons, the next stage is to challenge students to identify and respond to the counter-arguments to their beliefs. Dialectic involves the pursuit of truth by means of confronting argument with counter-argument, and as such it is central to the process of enquiry in any setting. Go to a court of law, to a legislative body, to a scientific laboratory, to a film production unit, and you will find dialectic at work in lively exchanges between opposing views. It is the tool we employ to refine our ideas, stripping out elements of subjective bias with the aim of achieving objectivity.

Some students confuse dialectical argument with a simple presentation of pros and cons. A student might, for example, present a list of advantages and disadvantages of using different types of energy resource for electrical power generation. But this is not, as such, dialectical engagement. The dialectical element consists in the focused attention given to argument. In stronger dissertations, students are able to develop a central line of argument, in which a critical discussion of one idea is used to motivate another. To counter-argue is not simply to state a counter-point; it is to engage in a critical analysis of an argument, with a view to showing that it does not succeed in establishing what it claims.

In a further echo of the trivium, I advocate basing the teaching of dialectic on two classical sources. The first is the method that Aristotle advocated. He believed that, before stating a position, it is advisable to undertake a survey of the *endoxa*: the received wisdom on any given question (see Ackrill, 1981: 10). Before attempting to make a contribution of one's own to a conversation, it is wise to attend to what has already been said, particularly if those sayings include the best that has been thought or said on a topic.

Aristotle may be accused of being an essentially conservative thinker, and it might seem as though his methodology is too deferential. Where is the scope for radical thought, if the place to begin is with a sweep through the opinions of the intellectual great and good? Isn't there a tacit assumption that established views have some special authority, simply by dint of their being established? But the Aristotelian dialectical method does not need this assumption. It can be justified simply by the more modest recognition that if you are going to enquire into where the truth might lie on a given question, it makes sense to look first of all at what has been said by others who have thought about it. At the very least, it is possible that their ideas have some truth in them, and that is a sufficient reason to pay some attention to the *endoxa*.

Students who write a literature review should have in their hands the materials to provide a survey of the e*ndoxa*. I recommend that a brief 'opinion spectrum' is a good way to begin the discussion section of their project. As well as suggesting ideas for them to probe, it helps to think in terms of the spectrum of views. Where are the extremes? How does one view relate to another? If a student can map out the intellectual terrain and identify their own position on the spectrum, they are well placed to begin dialectical engagement, for they have a sense of where they need to direct their argumentative firepower.

Moreover, one effective technique for defining your own view is to proceed contrastively. A student may not quite know what they believe, but it might be clear to them that they disagree with other views, and this insight provides some boundaries within which they can further mark out their own position. For example, if they are arguing in favour of embryonic stem cell research, they might map out an opinion spectrum ranging between unqualified support for such research, through to limited use (up to 14 days, for example, as the law currently allows), to a complete ban. They may not be able to say precisely where they sit on the spectrum, but they may feel that they are somewhere between the extremes, and this is a sufficient basis on which to enter into a critical analysis of the arguments.

At this point, students can usefully draw on a second classical source for guidance about how to go about the dialectical process: the method of disputation. If you were a novice monk, turning up for lessons at the University of Paris in the 13th century, you might well find that the task for the day was a 'disputation': a formal debate in which you were expected to propose and defend some theological proposition or other. The significant point about a disputation, however, is that the trainee might well be expected to be able to argue in favour of propositions in which he didn't believe. He might be asked to argue against his own beliefs, say, by proving that God does not exist.

The insight underpinning the method of disputation is that, for a full appreciation of the dialectical strength of a position, it is necessary to understand it as it appears both to its supporters and opponents. Someone who can imaginatively enter the mental world of those who disagree with their beliefs is far better placed to go about arguing persuasively with them.

The impact of this type of training can be seen in the philosophical writings of Thomas Aquinas. He begins his famous Five Ways (a set of arguments for the existence of God) by first putting the counter-argument. It seems as though God does not exist, says Aquinas, thereby immediately attracting the attention of his unbelieving readers, and provoking the believer. Their attention grabbed, he remarks that, when we look more closely, we find that there are compelling reasons for believing that He does exist.

Beginning with a statement and critique of counter-arguments makes good psychological sense. If someone sets out to persuade me of the truth of a proposition with which I disagree, I will not listen openly; I will be looking for the holes in their argument, convinced that they must be wrong. If, on the other hand, someone begins by showing me that there are problems with my view of things, I will be more ready to listen when they begin making a positive case for their own beliefs.

I therefore advise students, when setting out their arguments, not to begin with a presentation of arguments for what they believe, but with a critique of the arguments in favour of opposing positions. To return to the example of stem cell research, if they intend to argue in favour of regulated research, they could begin by critically evaluating arguments for a blanket ban, as well as those supporting unregulated research. Once they have dealt with these arguments, they could allow their position to emerge as a sensible alternative.

Few students find dialectical writing easy. As a rule, students prefer to assemble arguments that they have encountered in their research, rather than engage in the argument themselves. They tend, that is, to produce extended literature reviews, in which they describe arguments rather than pitching into the debate. A certain amount of training is required to get students into the habit of argument, and it is here that the taught-course element of an EPQ programme pays dividends, by familiarizing students with the practice of engaging in discussion and debate.

What, though, of the many students whose EPQs take the form of practical projects (the production of a performance or creation of an artefact)? Has dialectic a role to play here? Indeed it does. The development process should involve the application of dialectic to the practical challenges of project development. That is to say, the student's decisions about what they make or perform should be the result of a process of critical reflection about the relative merits of different ways of realizing their creative intentions. The creative journey should be driven by reasoning. The type of reasoning employed in practical projects differs from the type used in theoretical projects. With practical projects, the reasoning aims at action, not theoretical conclusions.

Following initial research, an array of different creative avenues will lie open to the student, and during the development of their project, they will explore these, evaluating how well they can achieve their objectives by proceeding down these different routes. Is one scene from *Hamlet* more suitable than another to perform before a young audience? Will the performance be more effective if it is set in one era rather than another? What do we mean by an 'effective' performance? (The philosophical element is never far away!) What effect is the performance intended to have on the audience? These questions will involve an ongoing reflective journey, in which argument and counter-argument take place, not between different theories, but between different creative options.

Dialectic therefore provides an underpinning, unifying structural feature of successful project work, whether it takes the form of a written defence of a proposition, or a creative realization of a practical design brief or performance. Whether the case is made out of wood or out of words, the essential process of creativity through dialectical argument between alternative possibilities remains the same.

Here again, we find congruence between the pedagogy underpinning successful Extended Project work and the principles of the trivium. In the opening chapter of *Trivium 21c*, Martin Robinson explains his view that creativity emerges within the context of a disciplined, structural framework. His drama students were taught a specific method of developing their work. This, rather than 'free' expression of their own initial thoughts or feelings, led to performances with depth and meaning.

The same is true of successful EPQs. These typically emerge from a carefully designed process in which there is structured support for the essential aspects of the process – namely planning, research, development and review. Moreover, within each of these phases, depth is achieved via the deliberate teaching of the necessary skills, with a focus on philosophical reasoning processes such as the clarification of ideas, the exploration of meaning, and a focused attention to the dialectical logic of the creative process.

The Oral Presentation: A Rhetorical Flourish

For the vast majority of EPQ students, the climax of their project is an oral presentation of their work to an audience typically consisting of teacher-assessors and the student's peers. The presence of an assessed oral presentation within the EPQ is a reflection of the significance that attaches to rhetoric. Rhetoric, understood in Aristotelian form, is the stylistically effective (and at times passionate) presentation of the logical support for a point of view, and thus an EPQ presentation is the rhetorical flourish with which the project process ends.

In the model of independent learning that underpins the EPQ, the achieving of independence happens as the result of a managed process, and the oral presentation constitutes its culmination. It is the point at which the seeds that were sown during the initial philosophical conversations, which grew through the process of research and development of ideas, now flower. In many cases, by the time they are ready to present, students have become 'mini-experts' on their topic of research, and the oral presentation is an exciting (if daunting) opportunity for them to demonstrate the extent and depth of their understanding.

The Philosopher Kid Grows Up

At its best, an EPQ is not just a dry run for a university dissertation, but is also a journey of personal exploration; a means of gaining the Socratic wisdom that comes through having seen a problem or issue through the lens of alternative perspectives. Through such awareness, a degree of intellectual caution is engendered – not a sceptical suspension of judgement but a qualification of it. This is the sort of journey that Socrates would have identified as a movement towards wisdom – the wisdom that comes with appreciating that widening the circle of our knowledge brings with it a greater awareness of its limitations.

In the EPQ, this is shown through the evaluation of the project, where students are encouraged to reflect honestly and in depth about the gaps in, and limitations of, their work. As I say to students, with gentle irony, many of the questions they have posed in their research have been discussed for thousands of years before they made their contribution, and it is possible that there remains more to be said. It is impressive when a student has gained not just knowledge, but the wisdom that comes with appreciating the limits of their knowledge, and in the best evaluations, rather than glossing over gaps in arguments, or structural difficulties in their work, students address such weaknesses directly and explicitly.

At Highbury Grove School, as a result of reflection on the principles of Trivium 21c, Plato's concept of the philosopher king has been transmuted into the pedagogical ideal of the philosopher kid:

> Philosopher kids are curious to know, question, and they can lead as well as follow. Philosopher kids like to feel, to think, and are notable for their eloquence and ability to take part in the 'great conversation' through which they make a contribution to our common life. Philosopher kids engage thoughtfully in dialogue and argument, they appreciate and make beautiful things, they are confident when grappling with difficult ideas, they love music and also seek out space for quiet reflection and contemplation. (Highbury Grove, 2015)

There is more than an echo here of the values and principles of philosophical education that underpin the EPQ. The best EPQs are journeys of personal development: journeys that begin with philosophical questioning, progress into enquiry, and result in an increase in both knowledge and Socratic wisdom. In a nutshell, a great EPQ happens when a philosopher kid grows up.

References

Ackrill, John L. (1981) *Aristotle the Philosopher*. Oxford: Oxford University Press.

Bonnell, Joe, Copestake, Phil, Kerr, David, et al. (2010) 'Teaching Approaches that Help to Build Resilience to Extremism Among Young People'. Available at: www.gov.uk/government/uploads/system/uploads/attachment_data/file/182675/DFE-RR119.pdf.

Highbury Grove (2015) 'The Highbury Grove School Framework for Teaching and Learning'. Available at: www.highburygrove.islington.sch.uk/curriculum/teaching-learning/framework-for-teaching-learning/.

Higton, John, Noble, James, Pope, Sarah, et al. (2012) 'Fit for Purpose? The view of the higher education sector, teachers and employers on the suitability of A levels'. Available at: www.gov.uk/government/uploads/system/uploads/attachment_data/file/377930/2012-04-03-fit-for-purpose-a-levels.pdf.

Hume, David (1990 [1779]) *Dialogues Concerning Natural Religion*, Martin Bell (ed.). London: Penguin Classics.

Levinson, Ralph, Hand, Michael and Amos, Ruth (2008) 'A Research Study of the Perspectives on Science AS Level Course'. Available at: www.york.ac.uk/media/educationalstudies/documents/curriculumprojects/A%20Research%20Study%20of%20the%20Perspectives%20on%20Science%20AS%20finalmod%206june_Word_logominor%20change.pdf.

Locke, John (1975 [1689]) *An Essay Concerning Human Understanding*, Peter H. Nidditch (ed.). Oxford: Oxford University Press.

Nagel, Thomas (1974) 'What is it like to be a bat?', *Philosophical Review*, 83(4): 435–450.

Robinson, Martin (2013) *Trivium 21c: Preparing Young People for the Future with Lessons from the Past*. Carmarthen: Independent Thinking Press.

Rodeiro, Carmen, Sutch, Tom and Zanini, Nadir (2015) 'Progressing to Higher Education in the UK: The effect of prior learning on institution and field of study', *Research Matters: 10th Anniversary Edition*. Available at: www.cambridgeassessment.org.uk/Images/255867-research-matters-20-summer-2015.pdf.

Truss, Elizabeth (2012) 'Institute of Education Open Lecture on A Level Reforms'. Available at: https://www.gov.uk/government/speeches/institute-of-education-open-lecture-on-a-level-reforms.

Index

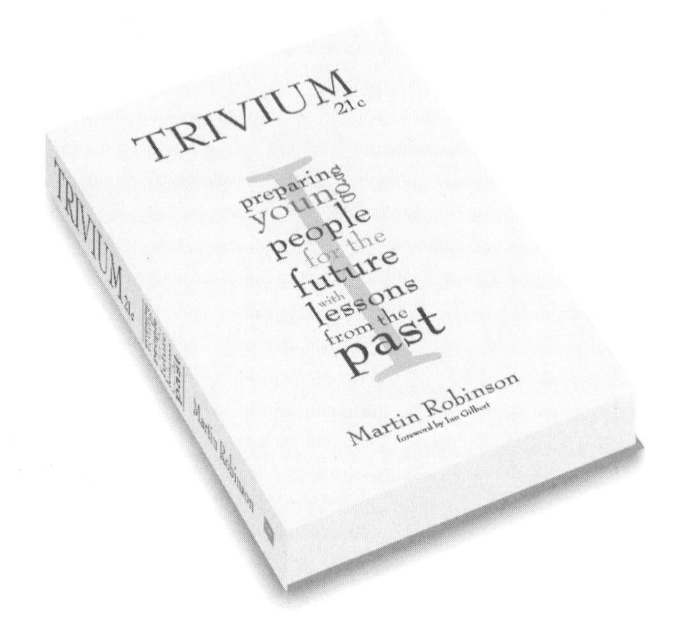

Trivium 21c

Preparing Young People For The Future With Lessons From The Past

ISBN: 9781781350546

From ancient Greece to the present day, *Trivium 21c* explores whether a contemporary trivium (grammar, dialectic, and rhetoric) can unite progressive and traditionalist institutions, teachers, politicians and parents in the common pursuit of providing a great education for our children in 21st century.